THE FLIRT COACH'S SECRETS OF ATTRACTION

By the same author:

Flirt Coach
The Flirt Coach's Guide to Finding the Love You Want
The Little Book of Flirting

peta heskell

THE FLIRT COACH'S SECRETS OF ATTRACTION

Develop Irresistible Pulling Power in All Areas of Your Life!

Element
An Imprint of HarperCollins*Publishers*
77–85 Fulham Palace Road
Hammersmith, London W6 8JB

The website address is: www.thorsonselement.com

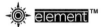

and *Element* are trademarks of
HarperCollins*Publishers* Limited

Published by Element 2004

10 9 8 7 6 5 4 3 2 1

© Peta Heskell 2004

Peta Heskell asserts the moral right to
be identified as the author of this work

A catalogue record for this book
is available from the British Library

ISBN 0 00 717572 8

Printed and bound in Great Britain by
Martins The Printers, Berwick upon Tweed

If I can stop one heart from breaking, I shall not live in vain;
If I can ease one life from aching, or cool one pain, or help one
    fainting robin unto his nest again,
I shall not live in vain.

Emily Dickinson

The teacher and the taught together create the learning.

To Joseph Riggio. You have guided me on my journey, you have shown me my own wonder and you have revealed to me my splen-door. And I'm still cooking.

CONTENTS

ACKNOWLEDGEMENTS

Once again Lizzie Hutchins, my copy editor, has weaved her magic on my meanderings and turned them into concise, meaningful prose and kept me amused with her comments. Many thanks to Carole Tonkinson for commissioning this book and for nurturing me.

I couldn't have written this without all my wonderful coaching clients and the people from all over the world who have been on my courses.

A big hug to Paul, my partner, who has taught me so much about chilling out and going with the flow and expecting things to work out. Thanks to his encouragement, I finally passed my motorbike test at the fifth attempt, while still working on this book!

A big thank you to my brilliant girlfriends Pammie, Patrice, Mary, Judith, Karen, Leigh, Alex, Lesley, Vivien and Nicky, who have inspired, amused and supported me as well as being the source of so many juicy stories.

A special smile to Paul and Rita, my first flirting couple; and Jackie, Martin and baby Thomas, living proof that this stuff really works.

There have been many amazing teachers who have influenced me and sparked off ideas in me and helped me along the way, but in particular two men stand out as major forces in my development:

Joseph Riggio, my mentor, and creator of the Mythoself™ process, which flows through all my work, including this book.

Richard Bandler, creator of NLP, whose genius has inspired and enthused me.

I owe much to the kindness and gentle spirit of Julie and Rupert Soskin, of the School of Insight and Intuition, and to Stacey Hall and Jan Brogniez for their work on synchronicity and attraction and the morale-boosting daily tips.

I would like to give a special thank you to the Mythogods, Des, Josie, Jeff, Lauren, Doctor Dave, Mike and Charlie. Long may the work continue. And a final thanks to Coen, and all the members of the Eurocoach list, for your inspiration and help.

And last but not least, thank you to all of you wonderful people who have given your time to assist on my trainings. I couldn't do it without you. Thank you, Adrian (seduction master), Caroline (laughter leader), Steve, (hunky biker coach), Nic (sexy fizz), Joy (keeper of the high), Jilly (Ms Super Smile), Patrick (Gallic love god), Richard (hunky tantra coach), Mike (meditation mythoman), Michael (infusing sexual energy), Sam (walk tall power), Telea (financial genius), Pixie (playful fun), Josh (timeline king) and Rachel (hot massage).

THE GENESIS OF ATTRACTION

Would you like to be truly attractive in all areas of your life? Sounds great, doesn't it? But do you really know what true attractiveness is?

Truly attractive people draw endless 'abundance' into their lives. They easily find love, sex and relationships that are just right for them; they love the work they do and even if they aren't millionaires, they consider themselves rich beyond measure. We wonder at the magical qualities they seem to possess. And most of us want some of the magic for ourselves.

We can have it. Each of us can radiate our unique powers of attraction into the world. Yes, that means *you* too. This book will show you how.

I have spent the last 16 years working on my own personal development and coaching many other people as well. As I began to be my true self, to speak openly and honestly to many people in my writing and to fully embrace my purpose, I realized that it was drawing very special people into my sphere, people who were helping me expand beyond measure. I began to work with my clients in the same way, helping them build up their inner resources and have a true sense of who they were. And the more they did this, the more successful they were at magnetically attracting great careers, good friends and well-matched lovers. They became more alluring in every area of their lives.

The key to being attractive is to allow yourself to shine in all areas of your life. This includes getting to know who you really are, finding your sense of purpose, harnessing your boundless energy, becoming more loving and loveable, having a sense of connection to other people and developing a powerful set of communication skills. When you are like this you will begin to attract more and more of what's right for you, whether it's love, sex, friendship, a happy family or success in your career.

So, if you're looking to attract a new job or improve your social life or find romance *and you're ready to take the leap*, read on. Here's a taster of what lies ahead:

The Mythology of Attraction: Before we get into the factors that make up a truly attractive person, we're going to look at some of the common myths about attraction. We'll be examining physical, chemical and traditional romantic attraction, and what lies behind it all.

The Heart and Soul of Attraction: Truly attractive people have what I call 'heart and soul'. In this chapter you will begin to tune in to your emotions and learn how to understand other people's emotions too. You will discover the power of living in the present, connecting to others, paying attention to your gut reactions and letting go of unhelpful thoughts.

The Power of You: Here you will go beyond the boundaries of primitive attraction to develop the confidence and self-esteem that are the most powerful attraction factors of all. You will begin to enjoy who you really are, unleash your own power and develop your unique 'Attraction Quotient'.

The Lure of Purpose: If you are looking to find the work that works for you and makes each day a joy to begin, read this chapter. You will learn how to uncover your life purpose and turn work into play!

Enticing Energy: This chapter is full of ideas on how to harness the power of your voice and body to transmit your own enticing energy into the world.

Charismatic Communication: Charismatic communication is one of the most potent attraction factors of all. Become privy to the secrets of charismatic people who just seem to have the knack of 'spot-on' communication.

Attraction Action: This is your personal 'Attraction Integration Plan'. It will draw together everything you've learned and provide activities to get you going on the path to being truly attractive.

Resources: And if after reading this book you're already thinking, 'What's next?' I provide a comprehensive list of tried and tested books, tapes and courses that will complement what you've already done as well as introduce you to a whole host of new ideas. And there are full details of private coaching and classes with me. I guarantee you will be inspired.

Of course there will be things in this book that will not be for you, as well as things that will leap out and speak to you. Take what works for you and leave the rest for the time being. You may find yourself coming back to it. And when you put your mind to it, and let the stories speak to you, and work through the explorations, you will discover that you have the power to become attractive in ways you might not even have imagined yet!

If you take one thing from this book that helps you to realize just how attractive you are or what potential you have, then I've done what I set out to do. But I warn you, there's a catch: *you have to be ready and you have to want to reach the essence of who you really are and what you really desire …*

If you are, then take a deep breath, let it out slowly, smile, allow the excitement to bubble up and prepare yourself to accompany me on a journey to release your own unique and lifelong powers of attraction.

When you're ready, let's go!

CHAPTER 1

THE MYTHOLOGY OF ATTRACTION

The hardest challenge is to be yourself in a world where
everyone is trying to make you be somebody else.

e e cummings

What is attraction? What makes someone attractive? Some of the ideas we've
learned to accept about attractiveness are leftover primitive programs from way
back which linger in our minds as some kind of 'how life is' story. Some of the
ideas are ones which our upbringing and environment have instilled in us and
which may or may not be right for us. And some of the things we believe about
ourselves are based on these ideas. It's no wonder so many people don't realize
their full attraction potential. The time has come to let go of old ideas and allow
in new ones that work for us ...

Physical Attraction

Far too many of us are hung up on the idea that physical beauty is what makes
someone attractive and that without it there is no hope. It is true that much is
made of physical beauty, yet it is a very shallow truth. We're led to believe that
beauty will make our life work. But it won't. Otherwise why do so many
beautiful people turn to drink and drugs? Why do so many people who have
cosmetic surgery still feel unhappy? Physical beauty is *not* the answer. And as
long as we continue to think it is we'll never learn how to be truly, deeply
attractive.

But before we get into that, a word about chemical attraction.

Chemical Attraction

'Chemistry' between people does exist and there's an explanation for it: we all have an inbuilt mechanism designed to help us produce strong and healthy offspring. It's as old as our DNA, but we are making new discoveries about it.

Through genome mapping we now know that everyone has a genetic predisposition to various diseases. Our genes are also designed to transmit imperceptible messages about their make-up to other genes. While we're looking around a room, our genes are busy sniffing out good matches. A good match is a genetic set that has different predispositions. A genetic set with a weak heart make-up is on the lookout to pair up with a genetic set with a strong heart disposition and so on. When our genes detect significant matching sets, they send out pheromones. Pheromones are chemicals that generate feelings of desire. That's when our gaze suddenly alights on someone across the room and we are attracted to them.

There is absolutely nothing we can do to control this level of attraction. However, it is useful to be aware of how it works. Being aware that you will be subject to seemingly uncontrollable urges may help you to stop and think before you take them a step further! I hope that it will also serve to remind you that we can't all be attractive to everyone. Take a look around next time you're out in a social situation. Do you fancy everyone in the room? Would you like to be close friends with everyone in the room? Would working with some of these people be your ideal? Would you be happy having all of these people at an intimate dinner party? Of course not. And they feel the same way about you.

Being attractive isn't about attracting everyone; it's about attracting *the people who are right for you.*

Traditional Romantic Attraction

Most of us are aware of the traditional qualities that men and women look for in a romantic encounter. Whilst these factors do come into play, they are very general. It seems to me that there are two different types: those qualities we are irresistibly drawn to in the short term and those we look for in a long-term relationship.

At the base level men are primed to spread their seed far and wide. In other words, in the short term, men are attracted to any woman who will willingly and easily have sex with them. They are on the lookout for any signs of sexual availability. So, to attract a man in the short term, all a woman has to do is wear sexually enticing clothing, touch herself as she's looking suggestively at him, smile, pout, lick her lips, breathe deeply, flare her nostrils and make long-lasting eye contact. These actions all have a direct effect on a man's sexual arousal centre. He will find them difficult to resist.

In a long-term relationship, however, men often don't want the qualities that attracted them in the first place. What *do* they want?

- *Fidelity.* In primitive terms, once the man has his woman he has to make sure no one else gets to her, otherwise how can he be sure the offspring are his? This might seem a bit ridiculous nowadays, but it's useful to be aware of this primitive trait in men. It's a fact that men get more upset about sexual infidelity whereas women are more jealous about their men confiding in another woman.
- *Support.* Men want a woman to give them support. They need someone who will tell them they're good at what they do, be there for them and constantly polish their ego.
- *A good mother.* Men want someone who will nurture their line. After all, there's no point having a line if it isn't looked after. This will be an unconscious factor for many men and it will depend how dominant their need is to reproduce. This tends to increase as men get older and think about what having children might mean.

As for women, what do they look for? Money and possessions are signs that a man has the means to provide (although they don't guarantee he will be willing to do so!) So if a man drives a flash car or lives in an expensive part of town or has a well-paid job, he's got more chance of being attractive to women at a surface level. I recently worked as a dating coach on a TV show where we were helping two rich guys who 'had it all' to find the one thing they didn't have: a long-term relationship. We advertised for women using the words 'Do you want to meet a millionaire?' We were so inundated with replies that we had to take on extra staff to cope.

Some women are also seduced by guys who are good fun and have a sense of adventure. They like the danger and thrills it brings. That's why bikers and guys who take on massive challenges or sail close to the legal wind are so attractive: they're thrilling to be with.

Other women fall for guys who arouse their emotions. When a guy gets out his guitar and starts to sing or pens a poem or pays them compliments, they go into meltdown …

- In the long term, what do women want? Nearly all women want a man who makes them laugh and is fun to be with. GSOH is the most common phrase in personal ads. There's something special about a man who can spark off those happy feelings. Laughter is a potent drug! And when people can laugh at themselves, that gives permission to others to laugh with them. Humour calms troubled waters, eases pain and turns situations around – definitely an ingredient for long-term relationships, wouldn't you say, girls?

- *Success.* Women like men who are successful. Success is symbolic of power. In primitive terms, powerful men protect mothers and babies. What isn't so great is what we've been taught to interpret as success. I remember how my friend Pamela's mother collared me, aged 14, to give me her 'finding a husband lecture'. She sang the praises of someone who was in a 'good profession' and was reliable. Needless to say, all her lecture did was to convince me *never* to end up with such a man, but for most women the reliable professional types do have a certain allure. What tells you a man is successful?

- *Security.* Some women, particularly if they've had an insecure family background with an absent or unloving father, go for the security of a considerably older man. This is often the 'perfect' co-dependent relationship. The man gives the woman everything she lacked in a father and she makes him feel young and in control. This is fine until the status quo is disturbed. The moment she begins to feel more secure herself is the moment she will need him less. His attraction may wane in her eyes as her security rises.

- *Reliability.* Reliability is also a quality women have traditionally looked for when they're thinking long term. At the primitive level, they are programmed to want a man who will be there for them and provide a stable home for the children. In modern terms this is sometimes translated into a man who is there in a crisis, who comes back home every evening and who joins them on the weekly supermarket trip. It's about protection.

These are just a few examples of things that people have traditionally been conditioned to look for. I believe that because we are all unique, what we need to attract into our lives are people, jobs and situations that are *a perfect match for us, not* what other people think would make us happy. That doesn't mean that they'll be perfect for anyone else. It's time to delve into what makes up that deeper, more personal form of attraction ...

Deep Attraction
LEVELS OF ATTRACTION

When you think of how you can become more attractive, several solutions may come to mind. You can categorize the approaches people take according to this model:

- You might be thinking about what I call 'surface' things: 'Maybe I should get a fast car, or hang out in hip places, or get a new wardrobe or hairstyle.'
- You might be thinking about the things you think you should do: 'Maybe I need to speak to people differently or smile more or touch people more often.'
- You might be thinking about the skills or abilities that you need: 'Maybe I need to brush up on my vocabulary or learn more about current affairs or get into cooking or learn to ride a motorbike ...'
- You might be thinking about what you need to believe and value: 'Maybe I should start to think everyone has potential or think about the quality of my life rather than the money my work is bringing in. Maybe it's OK to accept someone's untidiness if they have other qualities that are more important to me ...'

All these levels contribute to increasing your attraction factors. But what is really important is an even deeper level: the level of your identity. Who are you? What is your unique place or purpose in the world? And is your Attraction Quotient measuring up to your full potential?

Your Attraction Quotient: AQ

You've heard of having an IQ. That's when your 'intelligence quotient' is measured according to certain standards. But did you know that everyone every day is computing the *AQ* of everyone they meet according to their own unique criteria?

When you are in the presence of other people, you are *always* in their spotlight. You start out on centre stage and you alone determine how long you stay there. You determine whether they boo you off after a few minutes or give you a standing ovation. Every gesture you make, every word you say, every visual signal you give is being picked up by a part of their brain and processed according to complex criteria. And always remember that sometimes they will dismiss you from the stage simply because the match didn't happen for them. That's cool! They're not right for you, so move on to the next person!

So what are the qualities that you need to reach the peak of your own AQ? I studied attractive people and examined the qualities that they shared and here's what I discovered. As you read through the list, ask yourself this question: *How much more attractive would I be if this quality were fully developed in me?* And then smile, because you have the potential to develop all of these qualities in your own unique way.

What are the seemingly magical ingredients that attractive people share?

- They like themselves.
- They know what they want and expect to get it.
- They are happy and positively upbeat.
- They are confident without being arrogant.
- They don't *need* other people to make them happy, but people genuinely like them and actively seek their company.
- They are enjoying the adventure of their life, not just watching it pass by.
- They are successful and fulfilled in what they do, whether it's being a roadsweeper or a doctor.
- They are emotionally and spiritually mature.
- They have empowering belief systems that inspire optimism, excitement and determination.
- They have a strong sense of integrity and know what's right for them.
- They are able to be open and vulnerable because they have a resilient inner core.
- They sail through stormy challenges to calmer, more fruitful seas.
- They can laugh at themselves and life.
- They do things for other people without constantly thinking, 'What's in it for me?'
- They are able to surf the roughest waves on life's ocean.

- They see the potential in others.
- They speak positively of other people.
- They are loyal and caring.
- They want to see everyone win.
- They have well-developed social skills.
- They move and speak elegantly.
- They are exciting to be with.
- They are sexually mature and confident.
- They have an almost hypnotic 'follow-me' quality and make great leaders.
- They are highly flexible and can easily adapt to others without giving up their own sense of self.
- They are in tune with their intuition.
- They seem to attract what they want without effort.
- They experience 'failure' as a lesson on the path to success.
- Their bodies reflect all this with a sense of calm, a readiness for action and free-flowing uninhibited movement.

YOUR GREATEST ALLY

Reading this list may seem daunting, but the truth is that you already have the potential to be like this *and* you have a powerful ally: your own brain.

I would be insulting your brain if I likened it to the most powerful computer in the world. It's a zillion times more powerful. Your brain stores everything that's ever happened to you. You can learn to harness its power to create new beliefs, get a sense of your place in the world, learn about who you are and a whole lot more.

Your brain is constantly taking in new information from the world around you. It's processing and creating new ideas all the time. And sometimes it's reinforcing old ideas. If you can get it working at its best, you can become your best, most attractive self! So how does your brain work?

Your Brain Seeks to Prove Whatever You Tell It

Your brain takes instructions from you. It listens to what you tell it and then tries to prove it. When I worked at BMW as a freelance trainer, I was one of the few people who didn't own a Beemer. I would drive home at night and all I ever saw were BMWs. My constant thought was 'Everyone but me's got a BMW.' This simply wasn't true. But my brain heard that thought and picked out all the BMWs. And it just faded out the hundreds of other cars zooming by.

So every time you put yourself down or look in the mirror and you see yourself as too fat/short/ugly/whatever, your brain is being set up to find more evidence to substantiate that idea. But each time you say something *nice* to yourself or see yourself as having some *special* qualities, your brain is being set up to prove that too.

Your Brain Makes Links

Your brain captures every experience you have and stores all the information about that experience, including smells, tastes, feelings, sounds and images. It turns some of this sensory data, like a nice smell or word or voice tone, into triggers.

For example, when I was 18, I used to be crazy about a guy who wore a particular type of cologne. I bought myself a bottle and would dab it on my neck and inhale the smell and imagine he was there. Now, whenever I smell that cologne, it brings images of him flooding back into my mind. My brain linked a whole load of memories and sensory information about this guy to one single sensory trigger – the smell of his cologne. I bet you've got some triggers like that.

Your brain also creates triggers for unpleasant memories. Sometimes a fear of rejection or a feeling of being unattractive can be kickstarted by the smallest thing.

You can create your own triggers. Imagine how useful that might be. Say you want to approach someone and feel good about it. By bringing to mind and then 're-membering' fully in your body those moments you've undoubtedly had of curiosity, playfulness, anticipation, excitement, passion or other pleasant sensations, you can associate them with the thought of approaching someone. We'll look at how to activate this later.

Your Brain Has Multi-sensory Storage

Your brain can create all manner of images, sounds and feelings. You remember an image of someone being nasty to you, for example, and your body brings up the feelings associated with that experience. It works the same for the future too. Your brain is very imaginative. If you create an image of someone smiling at you and inviting you in, then your brain will create pleasant feelings in your body.

You are also capable of fine-tuning or brushing up on what your brain creates. An image might be bright, colourful, clear or fuzzy. It might be in colour or black and white. It might have a frame or be limitless. It might be moving or still. It might be happening around you or you might be watching it as an observer. A sound might be loud or soft, harsh or gentle. It may vary in pitch, timbre, tone and rhythm. You can make any changes you want. Try it out for yourself with this first exploration.

PLAY WITH YOUR BRAIN

Here's an opportunity to find out how you can direct your brain to do things.

- Make a picture in your mind's eye of doing something you enjoy. Even if you think you aren't good at making pictures, you might get an impression of it, in your body, with a feeling. This is good enough. Try changing the picture in some way. If it is in colour, for example, what would it be like if it were in black and white? Change its size. What do you notice?
- Think of a voice you like to hear. Listen to this voice as it speaks to you in your head. Try slowing it down or making it louder. Try changing it for a cartoon character's voice or the voice of a teacher who bugged you. Then end with another nice voice.
- Just get in touch with times when you got great feelings of satisfaction and remember how good that feels. And if the feelings start to happen now, smile because you did that to yourself!

You are in control of your brain. You can instruct it to make images and sounds and generate powerful feelings, and you can control the details too.

YOUR BRAIN FORMS HABITUAL PATHWAYS

Imagine smiling at someone you don't know. The first time you do it, your brain lays down a strand on a neural pathway. Every time you repeat it, your brain lays down another strand on the pathway. The more you do it, the thicker the strand becomes. And the thicker it becomes, the more of a habit it becomes. All habits are formed like this.

What nice habits could you use your brain to create?

EMOTIONS AND IMMUNITY

When you feel an emotion, it is because you have experienced something or had a thought about something. This causes your brain to generate a concoction of chemicals which flood certain parts of your body. Think of something you're dreading and notice how your feelings well up, where they're located and how they move around. Now stop that and think of something that really turns you on. You'll experience a very different type of feeling ...

The chemicals that cause good feelings boost your immune system. Those that cause bad feelings weaken your immune system. So when you generate thoughts about being unattractive, you are actually weakening your immune system. Learning to like yourself more and to develop deep attractiveness will improve your health *and* your wealth – and your self-esteem as well!

I shall leave you with the words of Norman Vincent Peale, one of the foremost writers on positive thinking. I've taken a bit of a liberty with them and substituted the word 'attractive' for 'succeeding':

> Formulate and stamp indelibly on your mind a mental picture of yourself as *attractive*. Hold this picture tenaciously. Never permit it to fade. Your mind will seek to develop the picture.

So come with me now and let us start to develop some true attractiveness from your heart and soul.

CHAPTER 2

THE HEART AND SOUL OF ATTRACTION

But you are the only person alive who has sole custody of your
life. Your particular life. Your entire life … Not just the life of
your mind, but the life of your heart. Not just your bank
account, but your soul.

Anna Quindlen

Those who truly 'have it all' aren't always the ones with loads of money or the
designer clothes or the hot babes or guys on their arms. They seem to have more
than that. It's as if they sail easily through life attracting the *right* jobs, partners,
friends and opportunities. Their partner might not look like a supermodel, but
they fancy them to bits. Their home might not be magazine material, but it's
lived in and comfortable. Their job might not be your choice, but it fulfils them.
They might not be living a conventional lifestyle or have a regular relationship,
but what they've got works perfectly for them. It's not that life doesn't hit them
full on and knock them backwards sometimes, but instead of lying down in
defeat, they pick themselves up and look for a way forward. They truly believe
that each knockback has a lesson for them. They also have the amazing power of
choosing how they react to events instead of letting them dictate how they feel.
They seem to have the keys to those secret doors of opportunity that appear
closed to others. And they don't just focus on making the most of their life, but
they also care about other people. They have a strong sense of the values that
drive them. They believe in something greater than themselves, whether they
categorize it as God or the universe or some other humanistic religious belief.

People like this are on their path and in tune with their destiny. Yet they're no more special than anyone else. They are simply in the process of realizing their full potential. And you can too. In this chapter we'll be exploring the qualities that are abundant in such attractive people and giving you a taster of what's to come in the chapters that follow.

One of the qualities of attractive people is that they have an elegant way of managing their emotions.

EMOTIONAL ATTRACTIVENESS

We all run a gamut of emotional experience. As situations come up we react by producing a concoction of chemicals that are transmitted to various parts of our body. These produce feelings that we label emotions.

What kind of emotions are your constant companions? Do you have certain ways of reacting to situations that make you feel bad or do you fill your world with positive sensations? When you become familiar with the emotions you experience and what triggers them, you can train yourself to do something different. Awareness comes before change. The following exploration is designed to make you aware of your emotional reactions to situations.

YOUR EMOTIONS AND YOU

Look at the following questions and just ask yourself, 'Do I ever behave in a similar way to this and what am I discovering about myself here?' There is no right and wrong answer. You're just observing your responses. You'll soon recognize what you need to pay attention to. There will be something valuable for you here, so be open to it.

1. **Your car won't start or you miss the bus. Do you:**
a) Start cursing and shouting.
b) Think about the dire knock-on effects of what's happened.
c) Accept it calmly and work out what's next.
d) Remind yourself to take better care of your car or be on time for the bus in future.

2. **You have tickets for an event and are looking forward to it, but your friend rings you at the last minute and cries off. Do you:**

a) Blame your friend, feel let down and resent them for 'ruining your plans'.

b) Go on your own and feel good because you aren't dependent on your friend to have a good time and anyway, you meet all kinds of people when you go out alone.

c) See it as an opportunity to invite someone else and have a different experience.

d) Pretend that it's OK to your friend and then stay home and feel sorry for yourself, secretly vowing not to rely on them again.

3. **You are driving in the fast lane at the speed limit and you notice a person driving too closely behind you. They flash their headlights at you. Do you:**

a) Get annoyed and hold your speed, saying to yourself, 'They shouldn't be going faster than this anyway.'

b) Feel a bit irritated and decide you'll hold on for just a little bit longer to teach them a lesson before you pull over.

c) Realize that they are stressed and move over as soon as it's safe.

d) Feel grateful that you don't need to take risks like that.

4. **You confide in a friend that you are romantically interested in a mutual acquaintance. A week later your friend informs you that they've got a date with that person. (You can just as easily apply this to a job you want or an idea you're working on.) Do you:**

a) Think your friend has betrayed you and refuse to talk to them.

b) Say that you hope they'll be very happy while secretly hoping it will all fall flat.

c) Feel momentarily angry, then realize that your friend probably liked this person too but might have been wary of admitting it after your 'confession'.

d) Tell yourself that if they're meant to be together then that's how it is and there are plenty more fish in the sea.

Think about your reactions to the situations. You may feel drawn to some parts of all of the descriptions. That's fine. Just be aware of your emotions and how they surface and how you manage them.

Which of these emotions do you hang out with on a regular basis:

anger	envy	regret	hope
nervousness	jealousy	grief	optimism
tension	spite	depression	joy
paranoia	greed	sadness	happiness
worry	self-pity	excitement	desire

Circle the ones that jump out at you and add in any others that come to mind as playing a regular part in your life. Be honest with yourself.

Developing Emotional Awareness

After completing this exploration, you might feel you aren't very emotionally balanced. You might even be at the mercy of runaway emotions! What can you do about this? Let's look at the secrets of emotionally balanced people.

Emotionally balanced people:

- recognize their emotions
- keep their cool and have a rapid recovery rate from setbacks
- are aware of the emotions other people are experiencing
- are able to help dissipate and work around other people's emotions

They know emotions are the body's reaction to thoughts generated in the mind. They recognize them for the signals that they are and act accordingly. They know that sometimes it's OK to have certain emotions but also know that it's not OK to wallow in them.

Don't make the mistake of thinking that emotionally attractive people don't get bad feelings. They do. The difference is that they pick up on these warning signs. And then they let go of the thoughts that triggered the emotion and focus their minds on what's happening right now. You can learn to do this too.

Here are four things that can help you develop your emotional awareness.

1. ACCEPT YOUR EMOTIONS

All emotions are valid. Fighting to suppress an unpleasant feeling will just send it underground and it will surface in some other, equally unpleasant way, often as a physical dysfunction. Instead figure out what thought processes created that emotion and stop thinking them! This chapter will show you how. First, tell yourself that right now you are doing the best you can. Acknowledge that you are eager to learn ways of changing how you feel and that your emotions will serve as a guide to help you improve.

2. UNDERSTAND YOUR EMOTIONS

Be on the lookout for emotional reactions. When they happen, ask yourself whether they were triggered by an event and what thoughts you were creating as a result of that event. Do this without censoring or criticizing your thoughts. Just notice them.

Recall how what happened after the emotion was triggered. If it was a negative emotion, did your thoughts cause you to spiral deeper into it or did you get out fairly quickly? If it took you a while to let go of the emotion, what were the knock-on effects to you and other people?

If you had bad feelings towards someone as a result of their actions, ask yourself how you can avoid being affected by them. Ask whether you think they meant to do it deliberately. Where other people are involved, *always check your evidence*. Sometimes we invent purpose and meaning for someone's actions by blending flimsy evidence into our own fantasy!

When you've finished, spend a few moments without judgement or regret, thinking about what you would have liked to have happened instead. What emotions would you have liked to experience? As soon as you are aware of that preference, formulate a statement about how you want to be. Write it out as an affirmation if you wish. Begin with the words 'I am becoming more ...' You could draw it or write it down somewhere where you'll look at on a regular basis or print it out and pin it up somewhere to remind yourself of it.

3. WATCH OUT FOR THE MIRROR

I was running to get to the front row of a seminar when I noticed a young guy passing me by. I said to myself in a ratty kind of tone, 'He's so pushy!' Then I had one of those 'oh, oh' moments. I realized that I was doing exactly what I was criticizing him for! We ended up sitting next to each other in our front-row seats. I tapped him on the arm and told him what I'd been thinking. I then added, with a smile, 'We're so similar, we're bound to get on.' We've been friends for several years now and I admire the way he's forged a really successful career at such a young age.

Sometimes we meet people and we dislike the way they behave. Maybe we experience envy or jealousy or some other unpleasant emotion. When you begin to judge someone, check whether you are judging behaviour or emotions that you exhibit too! Be brutally honest. Sometimes when we're not happy with ourselves we project our emotions onto other people. Research has even shown that people who hold on to repressed anger are more likely to be attacked by other angry people. So if you experience other people having emotions about you, it might be worth a quick check to see what you're holding on to yourself. You might be sending out vibes to attract people with the same emotions. Think about what kind of emotions you want to attract!

4. GET OUTSIDE FEEDBACK

Ask a good friend how they see you. This is an information-gathering exercise, so leave your emotions behind, be prepared for total honesty and decide that everything they say will be useful.

Ask your friend in particular what emotions they have seen you experience and what seems to trigger them. How does it feel for them when you get 'emotional'? Ask them what unpleasant emotion they've noticed the most in you. Get them to give you a 'map' of your emotional behaviour. Remember this is their opinion. However, there will be times when what they say resonates with you. Acknowledge it and be grateful that now you've identified it, you can do something about it. And don't forget to get them to tell you what they like about you too!

Managing your Emotions

Once you have a good idea of how you 'do' emotions and what triggers them, you can learn the art of balancing them and letting go of them.

Here are four things that you can begin to do to help yourself keep your cool.

1. TAKE RESPONSIBILITY FOR YOUR FEELINGS

When it comes to feelings, most of us have a tendency to lay the blame at someone else's door.

Melissa's husband left her for a younger woman. She had two toddlers and when he lost his job she had a pretty hard time. She spent a lot of time being angry with him and the other woman. She put so much energy into her anger and hatred that she hardly had enough strength to keep herself and the children going.

■ ■ ■

When Lewis's wife left him with three children and disappeared to 'find herself', he felt lost without her, but realized that he had to focus on making the best of things. Whenever he was tempted to feel angry with his wife, he knew that he had a choice not to feel like that. He told me, 'One day I woke up after a period of feeling really bad and said, "I'm fed up with wasting energy and time mourning something I can't change."' That was a significant stepping-stone for him.

Each time you feel angry or resentful or envious, no matter how much you feel someone else is to blame, say to yourself: 'I'm feeling this feeling right now and it's been generated by how I arrange the thoughts in my head. What other kinds of feelings would be more productive?'

It's not easy for everyone to do this instantly, but even just being aware that *you* are responsible for your own feelings shifts something inside you and makes way for different thoughts. What more important things are waiting to enter your head?

2. CREATE THE RIGHT ATMOSPHERE FOR POSITIVE EMOTIONS TO FLOURISH

Your emotional balance can be affected by your environment. Here are a few ways that have been proven to create a positive atmosphere for positive emotions:

■ There are lots of foods that affect your emotional balance. Sometimes an excess of sweet stuff and coffee can be your worst enemy, giving you an instant high and then dropping you down. It's best to drink a lot of water throughout the day.

- If you're surrounded by clutter, this is going to make you more frustrated. Clutter impedes the flow of calm and gets in the way of creativity. Clear the clutter from your life and you'll begin to clear the clutter from your mind.

- Make every effort to listen to music that calms you instead of watching TV all the time. TV generates all kinds of emotions and they aren't always good for us. Music we enjoy listening to generates emotions that *are* good for us.

- Get a water fountain that makes a noise and looks pretty when the water flows around it. The sight and sound of water have a very calming effect on people.

- Rest when your body tells you to. Most of us don't realize that we can only fully engage in an activity for about two hours, after which our energy declines and we're more prone to stress. If you can take short breaks of 10 to 15 minutes, you'll be doing yourself a great favour.

3. SWAP YOUR INNER CRITIC FOR A FRIENDLY COACH

Most of us are very familiar with our inner critic. Generally it consists of a voice, often unpleasant, that repeats nasty thoughts to us or demotivates us. It might be accompanied by some visuals, if you are the kind of person who makes pictures in your head. The critic's an illusion, yet it seems so real. It may have been a companion from an early age. Remembering that you are very good at creating illusions, instead of imagining the critic, why not conjure up a friendly inner coach to get you going?

You can create your friendly inner coach in exactly the same way that you created your inner critic. Here's how you do it.

INTRODUCING THE FRIENDLY COACH

- First be aware of how your inner critic works. Notice where the voice comes from and what it says to you. You will know what it says because it's often repetitive. Notice what kind of voice it has.

- That voice is out of tune with who you are and it's got to go. Play with turning down the volume or imagining it coming from far, far away.

- You can also try changing it to gobbledygook or a cartoon voice. Make the words so garbled you can't understand them any more.

- Notice if you create any images in your head while the voice is grating away. If there are any, stop them moving, shrink them down in size and blank them out. Turn off your inner TV, because you're about to have a very special visitor.
- Enter friendly coach stage right.
- Think of what you'd like your friendly coach to say. You have an unlimited choice here. The friendly coach can motivate you when you're down, ask you good questions that make you think differently, focus you on the positive, cheerlead you when you're doing well and challenge you to do even better.
- Pick a voice that's really appealing to you and have it say the words of the friendly coach.
- Practise your friendly coach voice as often as you can.
- Play with turning the volume up on the friendly coach and down on the inner critic. You can imagine you have a mute control button. When you press it, the inner critic goes mute. It's going through the motions, but you can't hear the words. As this happens you can have the friendly coach kick in.
- Experiment with using music and different coaches. After all, it's your experience. Make it just what you'd love it to be.

4. INSTANT CALM ON TAP

There are some marvellous techniques around for creating instant calm. It's useful to have a few on tap so that you can try out different ones in different situations. Here are two ways to instantly calm down. When you become aware of an unpleasant emotion rising up, you can use these to bring you back into balance.

CENTRING

- Pay attention to the spot a few inches below your navel. This place has many names because it's such a key factor in martial arts and Eastern body-management systems. I'll use the term *hara* for now.
- Imagine your feet are firmly planted on the ground and that you are sucking up energy from the earth.

- Imagine that you have a string pulling you up from the top of your head closer to the power of the sun.
- As you pay attention to your hara point, notice how much calmer and stronger you feel. You are more able to balance physically and you feel more centred. That's because you're focusing on the centre point of your body and aligning it with the top of your head and the bottom of your feet.

This is an amazing technique which can help restore confidence and bring you back into balance when you feel overwhelmed.

INSTANT MEDITATION

Some people think that meditation can only be done cross-legged in an incense-filled room whilst chanting 'Om.' And indeed that's how *some* people choose to do it. What you might not realize is that we've all done meditation naturally. If you've ever gazed at a baby or stopped to watch a puppy romp in the park or stood feeling the rain fall on your head or just stopped and stared at some beautiful scenery, you've been meditating. Meditating is simply the act of calming your mind and noticing what's going on right now, really experiencing the moment. It feels wonderful.

If you don't believe me, suck it and see.

- Sit somewhere comfortable, close your eyes and notice your breath going slowly in and out.
- Calm your mind and let your thoughts go. If you love water, imagine you are underwater and that when thoughts come up they just spiral up like air bubbles and float to the surface of the water. If you prefer not to use water, you can just imagine thoughts coming up and floating away into the air. You can imagine them going away into a container of your own choice to be stored for when you really need them.
- Try saying a word over and over. Some meditators chant a word or phrase so that they are focused on producing the sound and their brain can't concentrate on thoughts.
- Pick a way that works for you and don't set yourself any time limits. Notice how relaxed you feel and how calming it is.

SECRETS OF ATTRACTION

If you can only do it for one or two minutes at first, that's fantastic. Two minutes true mind-emptying meditation whilst standing at the sink washing up is worth more than 20 minutes sitting in the lotus position trying to meditate 'properly' and being plagued with thoughts about how to do it. Look out for places where you get the urge to just stand still and be for a while and follow your urge, if only for a moment or two.

Later I'll be introducing you to more mind- and body-management techniques which will build on this.

Tuning in to Other People's Emotions

> Do not treat others as you would yourself. Their tastes may not be the same.
>
> **George Bernard Shaw**

Have you ever been told 'Cheer up, it may never happen!' when you've been fine, just thinking deeply about something? This is a classic example of one person labelling another person's signals and getting it completely wrong. If you want to capture people emotionally, then you have to be sensitive to their emotions and their individuality.

NOTICE THE SIGNALS

When people experience emotions, their bodies react. Get into the habit of noticing these signals. Here are some examples of ones you might watch out for:

Visual Signals

His eyes crinkled up.

His mouth turned down.

He quickly licked his lips.

Her breathing became irregular and speeded up.

She sat up and let her shoulders relax.

She twiddled her thumbs.

He pulled his head back and his chin in.

He slumped forward.

He tensed his left hand.

Her lips turned up as if in a smile, but her eyes didn't change.

Her skin tone changed.

She flared her nostrils.

He looked from side to side.

She twisted her hand to the left and right.

Audio Signals

He spoke more loudly.

His voice slurred.

Her voice cracked.

She spoke more slowly.

His pitch got higher.

His voice slowed down and softened.

She used a monotonous tone.

When you pick up on these signals you might think you know what they mean. But even when we are certain we've got all the evidence, there's probably a whole heap more round the corner. Snap judgements like this can be dangerous, especially when we're 'reading' other people's emotions. 'Anger', for example, or 'jealousy', have really personal meanings and when we say to someone, 'You're angry with me!', we're not only judging them but also expecting them to understand our personal meaning. They might not consider themselves 'angry' according to their own personal use of the word and may feel indignant and misunderstood.

So, before you pin an instant label on someone's behaviour, *stop* and allow yourself to become curious about all the possible ways in which their signals could be interpreted. Let your imagination run riot. What myriad of things might be going on in their head? When you've come up with a lot of different reasons for their behaviour, you have set your brain up to look for more new ideas *and* been fairer to them.

Of course, you can always ask the other person what's going on. If you do, be sure to use vague open questions that give them the space to come up with their own explanations.

If you're on a first date, for example, or having an important meeting with someone and notice them looking at their watch or looking over your head, recognize the instant thought that comes into your mind (probably 'Oh no, they're bored!') and then *get curious*. You can say, 'I noticed you looking over there, is there anything on your mind?' or 'I noticed you looking at your watch earlier, how are you for time? Is there anything you need to do?' That's far better than saying 'Are you bored?' or terminating the conversation prematurely and unnecessarily. And you don't run the danger of planting a not very positive idea in their mind.

When Jane joined a new company she was introduced to Dominic. He didn't have much to say for himself and she noticed he seemed to be a real loner. She thought he was a bit stand-offish.

Then a friend invited her to a demonstration at the local karate class and she was surprised to see that Dominic was the teacher. She'd never have pictured him doing anything like that. Naturally she was curious and approached him after the class. After they'd got talking, Dominic told her that he'd grown up in the Far East and that most kids did some form of martial arts training there. When he'd started work at the office he'd heard the guys talking about football and drinking, and he didn't feel that they'd relate to what he did, so he'd kept it to himself.

As Jane got to know Dominic she realized that he had a lot of hidden depths that she would have missed were it not for that chance invitation from her friend.

STEP INTO THEIR SHOES

Sarah told me that what she loved about her new man was that he 'got' her. She loved the fact that he knew how she liked things and took it into account. When you can learn to 'get' people, it will endear you to everyone around you. To do this, you have to step into their shoes.

Successful salespeople (and by 'successful' I mean the ones who leave a lot of satisfied customers in their wake) are well versed in the art of stepping into someone else's shoes. When they meet a customer they don't prattle on about their product. Instead they pay close attention to everything the customer says and does. And they ask questions. Their sole focus is to pick up on what the customer might be attracted to and what they might have reservations about. Then they check whether their product is right for them, and if it is, they introduce it in a way that is right for that particular customer.

Similarly, when I run group workshops, it is my job to anticipate all the things that might run through people's heads when facing a strange and sometimes challenging situation. I also have to step into their shoes.

When you do this you are of course taking a giant leap in imagination, but if you've done your homework well, you should be able to make an educated guess as to how to approach them and what ideas might appeal to them.

Empathizing with other people depends on several things:

observation and signal detection
your own experience
information gleaned from good questions
your powers of deduction
remaining open to the unexpected

Next time you interact with someone, why not try it out? Imagine for a moment that you are in their shoes. How might you appear to them? What might you have said to affect them? What might they be afraid of or worried about? What might they want from this interaction? Keep asking questions and try to answer as if you were the other person. Don't just look for one answer, come up with lots.

This is a powerful talent to develop. And when you use it wisely it will give a positive boost to your attraction ratings. In the chapter on communication we'll be looking at this in much more detail.

APPRECIATE THE DIFFERENCE

When you pick up people's signals and step into their shoes, you will become aware of how they differ from you. Take this into account when communicating with them.

Allen was a very exuberant man. When he got excited about something, everyone knew. He talked loudly, made big gestures and generally exuded masses of enthusiasm. Marianne, on the other hand, was a quiet woman. She did get excited about things, but she didn't wave her hands around or shout and scream. When Allen talked to her about a new project he felt sometimes that she didn't understand how important it was to him. He accused her of putting a damper on the proceedings.

When Allen and Marianne learned that they each 'do excitement' in a very different way, they were able to make adjustments in order to communicate better with one another. Marianne learned to say encouraging words like 'Fantastic' in a louder voice and with more energy, and Allen learned to reduce the expansiveness of his gestures when describing something to Marianne.

A good way to practise this is to think of the other person as a car. Are they a slow Nissan Micra or a fast Ferrari? And depending on the answer, increase or decrease your own revs.

When you are mindful of the emotions of other people and able to show this in interacting with them, you will definitely become more attractive to them.

SPIRITUAL ATTRACTIVENESS

What do I mean by 'spiritual attractiveness'? Before you start imagining New Age airy-fairyness or religious sects, let me explain that it's just the way I choose to describe something you're very familiar with. You've probably met people who have many of these qualities.

Spiritually attractive people are grounded. They have a strong sense of personal power and self-esteem. They are open to loving and being loved. They rarely hide behind protective layers – what you see is what you get, because they are strong enough to let themselves be vulnerable.

Spiritually attractive people follow their intuition. They get hunches or they appear to have a charmed life. They have a code of ethics or values that guide them. They are aware of their actions and how they affect others and they don't let bad thoughts hang out in their minds! And they are generally engaged in some kind of activity, either full or part time, that they absolutely love.

Isn't that a nice way to be? Use the exploration below to get an idea of how spiritually attractive you feel.

HOW SPIRITUALLY ATTRACTIVE ARE YOU?

■ Just read through the descriptions below and then rate yourself from 1 to 4:

1. You have heaps of this quality.
2. You have quite a lot of it but a little more would be even better.
3. You don't have very much of it and you'd like more.
4. You definitely need more of this.

Quality	What's that like?	What kind of people do you expect to have around you?	How you rate yourself?
Connectedness	You belong. You may have a strong family connection or a supportive social group or religious group.	You expect to have people in your life who place great value on family and friends.	
Personal power	You are creative in your own way. You are aware you are a sexual being and you live life passionately.	You expect to attract people who will foster your passions and help you plant your power in the world.	
Self-esteem	You know what's great about yourself. You don't need other people to tell you you're OK because you are your own judge.	You expect to attract people who respect you for who you are and expect you to make your own decisions.	
A loving nature	You find it easy to forgive, commit, accept and trust.	You expect to attract people who are loving, open, trustworthy and committed.	
Self-expression	You are able to speak your mind and communicate clearly.	You expect to attract people who listen to you and are willing to understand you.	

Quality	What's that like?	What kind of people do you expect to have around you?	How you rate yourself?
Intuition	You trust your gut feelings and are a great judge of character.	You expect to attract people and situations that are right for you even if they're unconventional or not what you expected.	
Presence	You are aware of what you are doing and are ready to seize the opportunities that come your way.	You expect to attract people who are fully engaged when they are interacting with you because they've picked up on your special qualities.	

■ Now go back to the qualities you'd like more of and spend a few moments imagining what your life would be like if you could have more of them, Focus especially on the kind of people you would be likely to attract as a result.

Let's look at each of these qualities in turn.

Connectedness
THE POWER OF CONNECTION

All spiritual people feel connected. They rarely feel alone, even when they're on their own. Some people feel connected to the land they live on. They have a special relationship with the plants and trees and spend a lot of time in natural surroundings. Others gain their sense of connection through their neighbourhood or their families. They have a strong bond of love and loyalty with them and they feel supported. They take these qualities out into their daily life. Then there are those who have affinities with animals. They may get great pleasure from protecting or helping animals, but they also know that the animals give them back just as much. Some people feel connected to their work. They know that what they are doing has a positive effect on other people and that whilst they are following their own dreams, they are connecting with other people too. Whenever you feel a sense of rightness about what you are doing or where you are and can recognize the value you have to the world, you are connected.

How can you increase your sense of connection? And what will that give you? Come up with a list of ideas and just let them flow – even if they sound crazy! By not censoring yourself, you're freeing your creative brain. Here are a few ideas:

- Learn, learn, learn. Classes are a great place to meet people.
- Get online and join some communities. If you're looking for love, start connecting with people on internet dating agencies. If you're looking for friends, there are plenty of interest groups.
- Start a group of your own. I started an events group coupled with an internet list and brought in trainers for special evenings. I sent newsletters and put myself out there, and soon I got to connect with some very powerful people in my field and people got to know me.
- Network specifically. I joined a group called Women in Journalism because my business has benefited greatly from years of positive PR by friendly journalists. The first time I went to a meeting I made some great connections that led to me being offered two well-paid radio promotion gigs.

When you start to connect, a lot more doors open to you. And they in turn lead to other doors through which you may find people who are going to be very important in your life.

Mani was an Indian woman living in a suburb of London. She'd lived in her house for 15 years and out of 80 or so people living in her small road, she knew only seven or eight. She decided to give a party and invite all her neighbours. Over 60 people turned up and lots of new connections were made. Through that one simple decision on Mani's part, a neighbourhood community was created.

What was shocking to me was that this should be taken up as a news item by the national media. These kinds of get-togethers should be commonplace, not out-of-the-ordinary newsworthy oddities.

SECRETS OF ATTRACTION

Personal Power and Self-Esteem

Deep-rooted self-esteem and a sense of personal power are the foundations of attraction. That's why the next chapter, 'The Power of You', is devoted to helping you fully realize your own personal power and build up your confidence.

Love

A world without love would be a sorry world indeed. You know as well as I do how important it is to love and be loved, even if sometimes you pretend it isn't.

> Nick first experienced love when he was 17. He wrote love letters to Nancy and was overjoyed when she reciprocated. He enjoyed the feeling of being in love. And then Nancy ditched him. When another girl did the same to him in his twenties, he told himself that expressing love was painful. He learned to keep quiet and as a result closed himself off to love.

Yesterday I went for a walk in the woodland gardens near where I live. I stood by the stream facing some yellow irises. I was doing my chi kung exercises and the sun was shining on me and I felt great. And then I saw a baby moorhen chick float past squeaking for its mother. It was all fluffy and soft. In that moment I felt that extreme sense of unbounded love. It went right through my body and the world seemed utterly perfect. Love is all around for us to experience and enjoy, if we're willing to let it in and out.

When we feel love it's important to express it. Do you ever feel as if you want to tell someone you love them but something holds you back? What would it be like to let those feelings out?

> Annabelle's father thought that the way to show her love was to give her all the material things he could. She had all the clothes she wanted and a new car when she learned to drive. But her father rarely reached out to touch and hold her. When she instinctively ran to hug him, he'd shy away and say, 'No need for all that nonsense.'

Loving people reach out with and express the feelings in their heart through open arms and physical touch. Do you find yourself keeping your arms and hands to yourself or do you find it easy to reach out and touch?

Pat was not a man of many words. He found it difficult to say what he felt. When his partner asked him if he loved her, the best he could manage was, 'You know I do.' He also had a hard time being affectionate with her. For him sex was an expression of love. But because he didn't connect with his loving feelings, his partner said that it was as if he only knew how to have sex, not make love.

Sex has more intensity when it is driven by the heart. Take stock of your sexual encounters. What's the difference when you make love rather than have sex?

When you express your loving nature, love will be attracted back to you. Which brings us to ...

Self-Expression

The ability to express yourself is such a vitally important skill that I have devoted an entire chapter to charismatic and compelling communication (*see page 123*).

Intuition

The most attractive people are very much in tune with their intuition. This helps them to make better choices and go for the things that are right for them rather than those which glitter but are not gold.

We all get gut feelings, but all too often we dismiss them. Listen to your own messages, especially those that are suggesting you do something different.

Raj was single and fancy-free. One day he was on his way home when he heard a voice say, ' Go down the alley.' He hadn't used the alley shortcut for years. He turned into it. As he passed a shop, coming out of it was a girl he hadn't seen since he was at school. She's now his wife.

We've all had moments when we've known absolutely to go for something and also moments when everything inside is screaming 'No!' The first step to developing greater awareness, or 'intuition', is to calibrate our 'yes', 'no' and 'don't know' signals.

Simply remembering a time when you got the internal green light will bring it back into your body.

- Remember that time now and notice what your feel, what you hear and what prompts you to take action. This is your 'green light'. As you get in touch with what it feels like to get the go signal, get a sense of the colour green or a traffic light shining brightly. Next time you get the signal you'll be more familiar with it.
- Do the same for a red light signal, using a time when you absolutely knew that something was not for you.
- We don't always get a green or red light. Sometimes we get an amber signal. An amber signal usually means 'wait' and 'get more information'. Remember a time when you got an amber signal and become familiar with the feelings and where they are in your body.
Practise becoming aware of these signals in your everyday life and see how this makes a difference.

I've included some more exercises for polishing your intuition in the last chapter, 'Attraction Action'.

Presence
POLICING YOUR THOUGHTS

Thoughts are very powerful and insidious things. And not all of them are there to serve our greater good. Along with the good thoughts we generate gangs of hooligan thoughts which, if unpoliced, run riot and reap untold damage in our minds.

When you recognize the baddies, you can take evasive action. But most of the time we aren't aware of what we're doing until our thoughts have caused a reaction in our body and we get a bad feeling. The only way to catch them is to stay alert to them. At first you'll get the feelings before you realize what's going on in your mind. Then, as you progress, you'll start to pick up on a train of thought much earlier and before you know it you'll be able to change it for something better.

PERISH THE THOUGHT

When you do accidentally end up on a bad-feeling thought train, here's what you do:

- Focus your attention inside yourself and become aware of your body.
- Imagine you are at the movies watching your thoughts and emotions on a screen way in front of you.
- Accept the feeling is there.
- Freeze-frame it in the movie and make it black and white (if it is in colour in your mind's eye).
- Stop thinking about it.
- Don't judge or analyse it (because this is just letting another thought in).
- Realize that this thought, powerful as it may appear, is not part of your identity.
- Continue to observe what's going on inside you.
- Be aware of yourself silently watching your thoughts play out on a movie screen. Out there they no longer belong to you. You can blank out that movie screen any time and sit for a moment and enjoy being still and quiet.

As you do this process, you'll notice the feelings just disappear. And once the bad thoughts have gone, what nice thoughts are you making room for?

BECOME A ' NOW STAR'

Yesterday is in our rearview mirror, gone forever. And tomorrow is never promised to any of us. That leaves us just one day, the most important day, the only day that truly counts: *today*. This is our day to make a difference. But do you spend your time in the here and now?

George is deeply fascinated by history. He can quote facts and figures from all over the world and for years back. He eagerly watches programmes about history on TV and gets himself right back into the moment and feels the suffering. He also spends a great deal of time poring over his own history – a history of regret and missed opportunities. His favourite phrases start with:

'If only I'd …'

'I should have …'

'The stupid thing is that I could have …'

'If I'd known, I would have …'

He is constantly reminding himself of his mistakes and failures. And he believes that because something didn't work out in the past, there's no hope of it working out now.

Thinking like this is not very attractive. After all, who wants to spend time with someone who is more interested in what they didn't do than what's going on right now?

> When you hold on to yesterday, when you hold on to dead and dying adventures, you have no room in your box for greatness.
>
> **Ramtha**

For every George there's a Kim. Kim's friends call her Miss Worrybags. She does enough worrying for a boatload of *Titanic* survivors.

Kim says things like: 'What if it doesn't work out?' Lots of her sentences begin with 'might', 'could', 'may'.

When she comes face to face with a new opportunity, her first instinct is to come up with why it isn't worth doing and why it won't work out and what terrible things might happen.

Now a healthy injection of forward planning is necessary if we are to live and work with other people. But there's a big difference between 'Let's have lunch next Wednesday' and creating a future full of imaginary peril. That's seriously unattractive!

How about turning on to being a 'now star'? Living in the present doesn't separate you from your past or future, it simply puts them in their place. They do not exist. You can still be mindful of past lessons and aware of future possibilities. But just stay in the present moment. It's the only thing that's happening *right now*. And now is the moment to seize all those new opportunities …

RULES OF ATTRACTION

We all have rules by which we live. Apart from any laws or religious dogma we adhere to, we also have our own individual set of rules. These are our personal beliefs that we have developed during our lifetime. They may be anything from believing in karma (what goes around comes around) to a belief that you have enormous potential and can attract whatever's right for you.

We also all have a set of values. These are things that are important to us. They are often intangible and tend to be represented by big words such as 'freedom', 'autonomy', 'belonging', 'honesty', 'integrity', 'determination' and 'loyalty'. Values can also be defined as boundaries. We create limits for our behaviour and we won't go beyond those limits.

Sometimes situations create a conflict in our values.

> Henrietta loved her son dearly, but he was addicted to heroin. He was stealing from her and other family members to feed his heroin habit. No matter what she did, he wouldn't stop. She was faced with the 'tough love' choice: she knew that the only action left to her was to shop him to the police, but she was torn between that and her value of loyalty and love for her son.

When your values are in conflict, knowing what's important to you and what's *most* important will allow you to make decisions much more easily.

WHAT DO YOU VALUE?

- Think of something commonplace like a holiday or a job. Ask yourself, 'What are the key factors that have to be present for me to really enjoy this?'
- Your list might read something like this one created by Tina, a client of mine, who was trying to decide what was important to her about her job:

Being in charge of what I do
Having a change of scenery
Working with clients directly
The enormous salary

- Take a value, for example 'enormous salary', and ask, 'Is this more or less important than "working with clients directly"?' Depending on your answer, place one beneath the other.
- Take the value 'having a change of scenery' and ask, 'Is this more or less important than "the enormous salary"?' If it's more important, then ask if it's more or less important than 'working with clients directly'.
- Compare each one to the others until you have a hierarchical list. Your top value should be the one that's most important to you.

You may also discover that you value a material item because it gives you something much more compelling. Another client, Morgan, also earned an enormous salary, but he was very unhappy in his work. When I asked him what his enormous salary did for him, he told me, 'I've bought a big house and a red BMW.' My next question to him was: 'What does having the house and BMW give you?' He said it made him *feel powerful*.

The question 'What will that give you?' often provides very revealing answers. Often we value particular things because we've been taught they will bring us happiness, freedom, joy or power. These are what we are *really* looking to gain – and we may be able to gain them in a better way. My last question to Morgan was: 'As your greatest desire is not to have a car but to feel powerful, how else do you feel powerful?' This led him to thinking about personal power rather than power derived from possessions.

When you understand what you value and what it gives you, you'll find it easier to take the right path and follow your dreams.

Also, knowing what someone else values and what they value most enables you to understand them better and tailor how you present certain propositions to them – to make them appear more attractive, of course! We'll be following this up in more detail in the chapter on charismatic communication.

BACK TO BASICS

There are some things that we all need reminding of once in a while. Sometimes we ignore the simple things that can make vast changes in our lives – things like smiling, laughing, making eye contact and touching. You'll be surprised how many people *don't* do these things on a regular basis. My aim is to have you begin to do them regularly until they're second nature to you once again. Because then you're going to shine out as a very attractive person! There are a few other things you could try as well, and this next one is one of my absolute favourites. I was taught it by Kristen and Elsa, two remarkable ladies from Denmark.

'Yippee, I Screwed Up!'

What do you do when you 'screw up'? If you're like most of us, you'll probably have learned to have some kind of 'big' emotional reaction. You may wring your hands, scream or swear, apologize profusely, curse yourself for being stupid or want to run away and hide.

What if instead you were to jump up and down and raise your hands in the air and shout, 'Yippee, I screwed up!'?

Of course if your screw-up involves someone else being hurt, then it's probably best to tend to their needs first and keep your yippees in your head. But if it's something that only involves you, then learning to celebrate your mistakes is a powerful tool.

> Jens took this to heart. At the airport on his way home from learning to say 'Yippee, I screwed up!' he knocked over an entire stand of CDs. He said the staff were amazed when he started to jump up and down, screaming 'Yippee, I screwed up!' Of course, he also picked up the stand and apologized!

Celebrating your mistakes is one of the best tonics I know. You can always tell people that it's 'Celebrate your mistakes' week. This will explain your new behaviour and, I guarantee, someone will want to join in.

Celebrating your mistakes physically retrains your body to have radically different reactions from when you screwed up before. And if you are excited and positive, it's gonna be a lot easier to put things right … *and* people will be inspired by your positive attitude. That's pretty attractive, don't you think?

Smiling

If you see someone without a smile, give them one of yours

Your smile is one of your most powerful gifts, both to yourself and to others. When you smile you automatically create a particular concoction of feel-good chemicals in your body. And when you smile at someone else, their body is much more likely to feel the power of these chemicals and generate its own. When this happens they automatically start to smile inside – and often back to you. Isn't that nice!

Now you may say that this doesn't always work like that. You sometimes smile at people and they don't smile back. When this happens, what's your reaction? Are you annoyed at them or do you start to judge them or do you feel rejected? Remember you don't know what's going on in someone else's head or what situations they've just come up against. They might be so wrapped up in their thoughts they just don't notice your smile. If they're lacking in self-esteem or depressed, they might not believe that anyone would smile at them, so they won't see it. Some people just aren't ready to open to the niceness that exists in the world and they find it strange or they resent it. That's *their* stuff and that's where it should stay: with them. Focus instead on how *you* want to be and on what you want to signal to the world. Continue to smile and eventually you will get a positive response.

And when you do connect, and you wish to take it further, you can talk to the person with your eyes.

Talking with your Eyes

Before the words even come out of our mouths – and even if they don't make it that far – our eyes and our face are saying it all. That's why some people look away or down when faced with something that stirs their emotions. They don't want to show their feelings.

Our eyes are one of the most powerful tools we have for communicating with other people. We use them to glance in different directions to indicate an object. We use them in conjunction with the turn of our head or a gesture to invite someone to come over. We use them to indicate boredom, a question or disbelief, or to say 'I love you' … Sometimes we just make eye contact and send out a silent message. Lovers do this all the time.

We also use our eyes to bring back memories and access states of mind. When we cast our gaze in certain directions and we feel differently about things. Have you ever noticed how you look in certain directions when you feel bad? Just being aware of this can make you stop it and focus on something that generates better thoughts.

And once you're feeling good and you use your eyes to transmit those good feelings, your AQ will soar.

Try it for yourself. Next time you are on the bus or train and accidentally make eye contact with someone, instead of looking away or pretending you weren't looking, smile first and then look away. The chances are that the person will smile back.

You might also like to try the following eye exercises.

FRIENDLY EYES

Ask a friend to do this with you.

- Sit and look into each other's eyes. Notice what feelings you are getting inside. Notice what makes you look away.
- Try it again and this time in your head, without saying it out loud, tell your friend why you love them as a friend. Notice how that feels. Then tell them out loud what you were thinking. Discuss with them the effect this had on you.

■　■　■

- When you are out and about and you want to signal that you're available to connect with someone, look up, look at them and then look away. You might need to do this several times before they get the message!

LOVERS' EYES

If you have a partner, take some time to play lovers' eyes with them.

- Sit opposite each other, hold hands and look into each other's eyes.
- As you do so, just in your mind, not out loud, tell them you love them and tell them why. Tell them what turns you on sexually about them and why. Tell them anything you want, but it must be positive. Keep the eye contact.

You might get some pretty stirring feelings ... without saying a word. Go with the flow ... and make sure at some time to tell them out loud what you were thinking.

When you talk to people on a more formal social or business basis, too much eye contact can seem too intimate. The key is to keep it short but frequent.

In a more formal situation, make eye contact when you ask someone a question, when you give an answer, when you want to convey how much something means to you and when you want to show commitment. When people say 'Look me in the eye and say that', they are asking you for the ultimate verification of honesty – the chance to look into your eyes and read the truth.

■ ■ ■

The more you use your eyes to talk, the more you'll boost your AQ.

The Power of Touch

> Touch remains the most trusted connection between people.
> I will believe your touch before I believe your words.
>
> **Virginia Satir, family therapist**

In some cultures, touch is part of everyday life, in others it is reserved for intimacy. What do you feel about touch? Is it something that comes naturally to you? Is it something you want to do but you restrain yourself for fear of breaking taboos? Is it something you shy away from?

How you react to touch is controlled by how you think about it. If you think a touch will be sexually threatening, then it will be. If you think it will engender fear, it will. But whenever you allow someone to touch you, you are allowing intimacy. You are opening up and letting them in. So if you are a really 'touchy-feely' person, you need to pay attention to how your touch is received. Don't dive in until you've tested the water. Start the touch and then stop, notice if the other person pulls back, narrows their eyes or tilts their head a little upwards or their chin a little downwards. All these are signs that they aren't very open to touch. So take it gently.

If you're not very touchy feely and want to be, spend time watching people talking to each other and notice whether they touch, how often and where.

What other things do they do when they touch? Just have it at the back of your mind that you're going to explore touch and you'll be surprised at what happens. And the right touch can be very attractive.

Laughter – a Top Tonic

What was it like the last time you had a real belly laugh, when you laughed so much you thought your sides would split? Wasn't it fantastic? Just thinking about it might be enough to send you off again!

As children my brother and I were always playing outlandish pranks on our parents, our grandparents and neighbours. We developed the spirit of fun and it still runs through our lives today.

Now I'm not suggesting you play pranks unless you want to, but I am asking you to think about your attitude to having fun. Do you ever get silly and do crazy things just for the fun of it? When was the last time you had a good laugh?

Take a dose of laughter at least once a day – or take as much as you can and still live your life!

FIVE WAYS TO BUILD UP YOUR LAUGHTER MUSCLE

1. Laugh at yourself. When you do something stupid, bow to the people around you and ask if they would like an encore. Say something like 'And for my next trick …' Remember 'Yippee, I screwed up!'
2. Set yourself up for fun. When you get up in the morning ask yourself, 'How can I have fun doing the things I need to do today?'
3. Immerse yourself in laughter. Watch funny films or TV shows or go to a comedy show. Subscribe to a joke newsletter on the internet. Go where the laughs are.
4. Imagine you're laughing. Start by going 'ha ha ha' or 'ho ho ho' or shake your belly like you do when you laugh. Remember something funny. Soon you'll be laughing for real.
5. Do crazy things. Jump in puddles, talk to dogs in the park, wear your hair in an outrageous style, wear a funny badge or a T-shirt with a funny message, go into a pizza parlour and ask for a pizza with whole turkey legs or jam …

I'm sure you can come up with some more ideas of your own. And if you're stuck, come on one of my flirting weekends or join one of the many laughter circles that are forming all over the world *(see Resources, page 209)*. Your laughter muscle needs plenty of regular hearty exercise.

Remember that people who have a good sense of humour and who know how to laugh at life are really attractive. Is this you? If not, get laughing.

Being Strong Enough to Be Vulnerable

One of the things I've noticed about people over the years is how addicted we all are to protective layers. We spend most of our lives trying to cover up who we really are because we're scared that if we show our real selves, we won't fit in or be liked, loved or wanted. And then we run scared in case someone sees through our disguise.

When you're not scared to let your true self be seen, there is nothing for anyone to uncover. The key is to develop a core sense of yourself that's strong and empowering – and *attractive* – and then display it to the world without fear. As you do this, you'll realize just how many more opportunities seem to open themselves out to you and welcome you in.

If you are ready to unleash your powerful attractive self, turn the page and we'll begin ... with the power of *you*.

CHAPTER 3

THE POWER OF YOU

People are like stained-glass windows. They sparkle and shine
when the sun is out, but when the darkness sets in, their true
beauty is revealed only if there is a light from within.

Elisabeth Kübler-Ross

You are a mighty powerful person. You might not realize it yet, but your potential
is enormous! I have learned that anyone can be wonderful, magnificent,
awesome, amazing … When you acknowledge your potential, you are taking the
first giant step towards spilling your sunshine and beauty out onto the world.

A spotlight is waiting to shine on you. Only you can switch it on. And
when you do, it shines on everyone around you.

But first, it might be useful to be aware of how you rate yourself in the
attraction stakes right now.

YOUR ATTRACTION QUOTIENT

The first step on your journey through this book is to take a good long look at
yourself. Then, as you move on and begin to make changes, you can look back
and see how much you've gained and be proud of your progress.

As we've learned, whatever you're thinking, your body is reacting
accordingly. And body awareness is essential in helping you to pick up on your
own signals. If something doesn't feel good, you can do something else. If it
does feel good, you can do it more often!

As your awareness grows you'll also recognize the warning signs of a downward thought spiral. This is good because it means you can change it before it goes too far – unlike John.

John came to see me because he thought I could give him some tips on how to make himself attractive. He started talking about his life. He told me that his wife had dumped him and left him to bring up his two sons, and his mother had never given him any encouragement or affection. Then he told me that he was going to see a stylist the next day. This was followed by a whole list of reasons why she probably wouldn't be able to help him. Then he looked up at me and said, 'I bet I'm going to be your biggest challenge.'

I asked him, 'On a scale of one to ten, how do you rate your attractiveness?' He replied, 'What's the lowest number on the scale?' I told him, 'It's one.' 'Well,' he smirked, 'I'm a zero.'

It wasn't that I'd given up on him; he'd given up on himself.

John was an extreme example. And even if you may sometimes have had John-like tendencies, that's OK, because you're moving on, aren't you?

WHAT'S YOUR AQ?

This exploration is not one of those quizzes that marks you against someone else's standard. It is a powerful opportunity for you to become more aware of your body and of which thoughts trigger which feelings.

Consider the statements below and write in the box next to the sentence the score that best reflects your response to it. The scale goes from 1 to 4:

1. I strongly agree – this is very true of me.
2. I agree – I'm like this sometimes.
3. I disagree – I'm rarely like this.
4. I strongly disagree – this is not me at all.

It's in your interest to do this honestly and with the first response that comes up. I know it's tempting to think, 'What's the right answer?' But there is no right answer other than the one that comes up for you now.

This isn't a test; I'm not going to mark you. This exploration will simply alert you to the areas that need polishing.

Body-awareness Drill

Before you begin, focus your attention on your body and do a quick scan of how you are feeling, starting with the crown of your head and ending with the balls of your feet. This is to help you become more body aware so that you can benefit fully from the next part of this exploration.

OK, now on to the statements ... How do you rate yourself?

1. I think I'm a pretty fantastic person. ☐
2. I know I'll be highly attractive to the right people for me. ☐
3. I am a happy person and nothing much gets me down. ☐
4. I don't care if people don't like me because I know I'm likeable. ☐
5. I wake up every day and look forward to going to work. ☐
6. I know what's important to me and my values guide my actions. ☐
7. When I get a knockback, I brush it off easily and move on. ☐
8. I recognize that I'm subject to emotions, but I don't allow them to overwhelm me. ☐
9. I believe that everyone in the world is connected. ☐
10. In my own way I am destined for great things. ☐
11. I never speak ill of my friends. ☐
12. I find it easy to speak to strangers in bars or at parties. ☐
13. I don't regret anything I've done. ☐
14. When things don't go the way I planned, I accept it as the way it is meant to be and feel good about it. ☐
15. I expect delightful things to happen to me. ☐
16. I'm very sexy and desirable. ☐
17. People are positively influenced by what I say. ☐
18. My life just seems to work out perfectly. ☐
19. I am highly adventurous and open to trying new things. ☐

20. I look for the good in other people. ☐
21. I am the first person to laugh about myself when I've done something silly. ☐
22. I enjoy helping other people, but I'm not a doormat. ☐
23. When I don't want to do something I find it very easy to just say no. ☐
24. I don't feel envious of other people's success, I just admire them. ☐
25. I find it easy to attract money, friends and lovers. ☐

How did you do? Remember, the only standard you need to hold up to yourself is how you want to be. What would it be like to be more like that? Just a thought to bear in mind for a while ...

Check your Feelings

As we now know, it's really useful to be able to recognize how your body reacts to situations and how you generate feelings. Then you can learn how to do more of the stuff you like and less of the stuff you don't. This part of the exploration is designed to help you become more aware of how your body changes as your emotions shift.

HOW DO YOU DO YOUR NEGATIVE STUFF?

- Look at the statements where you scored yourself as a 3 or a 4. (And if you got a lot of them, take it easy on yourself – it's just useful information.)
- Read through the statements and think about how you are when you're *not* being like that. Notice any images you are making, anything you're saying to yourself, where the feelings begin in your body and what they're like. I bet that doesn't feel so good, does it?

HOW DO YOU DO YOUR POSITIVE STUFF?

- Now look at your answers and pick out the statements where you've scored a 1. Read each statement again and say it out loud to yourself. As you do so, become aware of any images you are making, anything you're saying to yourself and above all the different feelings generated in your body.
- Where do the good feelings begin? What are they like? Are they tingly, piercing, sharp, gentle, smooth ...? Where do they stop or leave your body?

- Keep reading the statements until you get a strong sense of the different ways in which your body does the positive stuff. This will be very useful to you later on.

And Finally ...

- Now, if you dare, ask a friend or partner to complete this form based on what they think of you. Ask them to be totally honest and be OK about whatever they say. It could open up some really great discussions and speed up your transformation!

THE LAW OF ATTRACTION

The Law of Attraction states that you can attract to you everything you need, according to the nature of your thought life. Your environment and financial condition are the perfect reflection of your habitual thinking. Thought rules the world.

Joseph Murphy, 1898–1981, prosperity writer

Imagine what it would be like if you could attract whatever you wanted into your life. Wouldn't that be wonderful? Or would it? It can have disastrous results, as King Midas discovered. He wished that everything he touched would turn to gold and then found that his food and water and his family also turned to gold. And, what you think you want might not turn out to be what's right for you.

Wishes are powerful things and unless we phrase them carefully, we might end up with something we don't want. When someone whines, 'But I so want to be rich,' yet says things like 'When I win the lottery I can do that', they are *not* going to win the lottery or get rich. You will see how this works later. On the other hand, when we allow our natural self to shine out and we wish carefully and with a win-win outcome in mind, we often get exactly what's right for us.

The Law of Attraction has fascinated me for some time now. It's pretty cool as guides go, but it's not a magic wand. Sometimes we wish for something like a new partner or more money and we don't get it. The Law of Attraction is not simply about wishing and getting. It's about getting what is right for you at that particular time in your life. It's about like attracting like. The more attractive *you* are, the more you will attract what's right for you.

Become the change you seek in this world.

Gandhi

Belief is important here. If you don't believe you are attractive, no matter how much other people tell you otherwise, you will find it challenging to accept what they say. If you are constantly telling yourself that you are ugly and that no one will like you, guess what? You will appear ugly and people won't like you. If you believe that you are unworthy or incapable of attracting what you want, you won't! If you see black clouds instead of silver linings, your life will appear to you as a series of dark events. Scary stuff!

THE EFFECT OF THOUGHTS
See for yourself how your thoughts affect the way you appear.

- Stand in front of a mirror and say nasty things to yourself. Pick out all your faults.
- Notice the changes in your posture and facial expression.
- *Stop.*
- Now stand there and say nice things to yourself, even if you don't believe them yet!
- Notice the difference in your appearance. Amazing, isn't it?

But it works in more subtle ways too.

Imagine for a moment that there is a central control centre that has the blueprint for you. It knows exactly what is perfect for you to blossom into the unique marvellous creature you are. This control centre is constantly reacting to you. It is aware when you're 'off print', not following your blueprint, and it does warn you, but it's quite subtle. Sometimes the warning is just a feeling or a voice in your head or a picture that flashes up. But when you ignore it, the control centre begins to attract things that will make you aware of it.

Your control centre is also aware when you're 'on print' and it will direct you towards the things that are right for you. When you take heed of the natural Law of Attraction, you always get what's perfect for you. And there are many ways to do this, as you're going to discover.

YOUR ATTRACTION JOURNAL

As you are about to experience some good feelings and positive thoughts about yourself, this is the perfect time to introduce you to the amazing power of keeping an attraction journal.

When you make changes in your life, keeping a record of the little milestones along the way can be most useful. It's also really great to keep reminding yourself of how attractive you are becoming.

It makes sense that an attraction journal should be attractive, doesn't it? So I suggest you find or buy a book that makes you feel really good. There are some lovely notebooks in the shops now. Find a pen that you really like writing with, or you might prefer to use your computer. Choose a recording method that you enjoy.

Hint: If you're an avid e-mailer, you might find some of the things you e-mail to friends are great journal material!

Using your Journal

Use your journal to write down any thoughts about attraction. Here are some questions you can ask yourself. Use them as a prompt to get your thoughts flowing.

What do you want to attract today?
What's your positive wish for the day?
What have you already attracted in your life?
Who or what did you attract today?
Who smiled at you or vice versa?
Who spoke to you and whom did you speak to?
What different things did you notice about yourself compared to yesterday?
What lessons or positive things have come out of something that didn't seem so positive at the time?
What was attractive about you today?
What little things have you achieved today?
What big things have you achieved today?
What positive thoughts have you had today? (They can be anything from admiring the colour of something to thinking about doing something you've always dreamed of.)

As you keep this diary, you are building up a storehouse of positive incidents that you can read whenever you need a boost. You are boosting yourself with your own success!

And the more you notice moments when you've felt attractive, the more you'll feel attractive … naturally.

A WORD ON SYNCHRONICITY

Synchronicities are events that some people label 'coincidences'. Have you ever been thinking of someone and they called, or been thinking of something and saw it in a shop window? From now on, be sure to pay attention to the synchronicities in your life. Instead of saying 'Just a coincidence' you could start saying 'Hmmm, interesting. I wonder what that signifies?' Soon you'll find all kinds of interesting things popping into your consciousness.

FINDING THE SILVER LINING

Finally, here's a word of warning: be careful what you write in your journal. Aim to focus on the positive. Even if you come up with a seemingly negative event, find the value in it. There always is some value.

For example, which of these statements sounds better to you:

Missed the bus this morning.

Missed the bus this morning but got to do 20 minutes' exercise/smile at a pretty girl/chat to a nice stranger …

Always look for the benefits. They will always be there, but sometimes you can't see them clearly at the time. You might like to write down the 'negative' event and then use the word 'but'. This word directs the brain to fade out what went before and focus on what came out of it.

The next exploration is designed to help you draw out the sunshine from behind the clouds.

Remember a time when you really wished for something and *didn't* get it? Somewhere, sometime chances are you've had that happen to you.

- What was it?
- Was it what you really wanted or were you trying to get something else?
- What stories or reasons or excuses did you create?
- What happened as a result?
- How can you turn what happened into a benefit?
- Is it a lesson about how to do something or is it a severe warning not to do it again?
- Did it lead to something more suited to you happening? Think about that.
- What did you gain from it? Did you really lose anything?

Quick Tips on Keeping an Attraction Journal

- Make it attractive so that you *want* to write in it.
- Decorate it any way you want.
- Before you write in it, spend a moment or two focusing on the questions above.
- Just write, don't edit. Let your thoughts flow.
- Do it on a regular basis.
- Focus on what's positive, useful and possible.
- Record whatever you think is significant.
- Re-read past entries and let yourself wander into a daydream remembering them. Go back and play them again in your mind.

DEVELOPING YOUR AQ

If I were to wish for anything, I should not wish for wealth and power, but for the passionate sense of the potential, for the eye which, ever young and ardent, sees the possible. Pleasure disappoints, possibility never.

Søren Kirkegaard

If you want to develop your magnetism and get what's really right for you, it is vital to boost your AQ. And once you do that, although you might have a particular issue in mind, it will spill over into every area of your life. What would that be like? Let's indulge in a little targeted dreaming for a moment or two.

Dreaming of a High AQ

Daydreaming allows you to build in your mind a very strong sense of what it is like to be attractive in various areas of your life. The richer you make the dream by evoking sights, sounds and feelings, the more real it will appear to your neurology. And you will feel familiar and comfortable with it when the time comes to realize it.

Developing your ability to daydream will create positive feelings which in turn will cause your body to emit positive chemicals and you will find yourself attracting all sorts of interesting stuff into your life.

DREAMTIME

Look at each of the areas of your life below and just allow yourself to start daydreaming. The questions will guide you.

Relationships: Love beyond Measure

What would it be like to be in a relationship where your partner found you highly attractive in many ways?
If you are in a relationship, how would that improve your communication, your sex life, your time together?
If you are not in one yet, what qualities would you find in your dream partner? What qualities would you have to develop to attract them?
Get specific and then dream. What might you find yourself doing, with your partner, on your own and beyond the relationship?

Career: Following your Bliss

You may well be in the process of getting a job, making your current job more fulfilling, building a business, going for promotion, marketing for new customers, expanding your business, working with other people, being in a team, being a leader, changing your image, quitting your job or starting a new venture.

What and whom would you have to attract in order to make this work?
How would you make sure that getting what you want had no negative effects on others?

Health: Vigorous Well-being

How might being a magnet for better health affect other areas of your life?
How would it be finding yourself taking on more healthy habits, just because they seem right for you?
What step would you like to take right now on the road to healthier living?
What will it take for you to just do it?

Finances: Absolute Abundance

Money makes the world go round. Think of a way in which having more money would benefit you *and* benefit a lot of other people.

If you have a business and are working on getting a major contract or cutting a deal where you will end up financially better off, what good would that bring to your life and the lives of people connected to you?
What kind of people do you want to attract as clients, employers, employees, colleagues?
What does having enough money in the bank mean to you?
What might be the difference between financial freedom, financial security and financial independence? Which do you want?

■ ■ ■

When you have finished, write down what you distilled from your daydreams. This makes them seem more real. A good way to start is to write:

As I become more attractive in my ... I ...

For example:

> As I become more attractive in my relationship, I notice more
> admiring glances from my partner, I have better orgasms,
> I feel freer to be myself. I am more joyful, I smile more
> ... etc, etc.

Now let's have a look now at some of the archetypal qualities we've taken on over the years and how they influence who and what we attract into our life.

ARCHETYPAL ATTRACTION

Partly as a result of our social imprinting and partly because of our genetic make-up we have generated different ways of coping with the world which we call archetypal. Much has been written about the different archetypes and it's useful to have an understanding of their characteristics and to recognize your own tendencies. This will give you a deeper understanding of why you find certain people attractive and why certain people are attracted to you. These archetypal patterns are as evident in friendships and business matches as they are in love relationships.

The Power of Archetypal Attraction

As a child of 10 I experienced a recurring dream. I dreamed I was a soldier. I would open the door of my house and across the road I would see a man with some kind of injury. Usually it was a broken arm or leg. I would rush over to the guy and fix him up.

At the time I had no idea of the dream's significance. Yet for most of my adult life I was attracted to men who needed rescuing in some way. I would put much of my energy into fixing them. This of course made me quite attractive to them. I would enter their lives like an angel waving a magic wand. I also found myself being the person people would call when they had problems. But because I was getting my satisfaction from fixing people, the danger was that they would lose their attraction to me if they didn't need fixing. For me to be happy they had to remain broken. I was the archetypal 'Rescuer'. What I didn't realize at the time was how big a drain these people were on my emotional resources. One person cannot live life for another.

Today, I would never use the words 'broken' or 'fix', because I don't believe people are broken and I don't believe I 'fix' people. I believe that everyone is perfect, with perfect flaws, in the same way that part of the value of a diamond is that it has flaws.

My hope is that in understanding what archetypes are predominant in you, you can begin to accept these characteristics not as impediments but as God-given tools that you can use positively to fashion a unique work of art.

Transforming Archetypes

Below is a list of some of the most common archetypes, giving their extreme features as well as the way they can be transformed to positive use. For example, I have transformed my rescuing tendencies into empowering others. When I work with clients I feel a sense of satisfaction from being a catalyst in their change. We all find ourselves expressing various degrees of our own archetypes, from the extreme to the more mellow.

If you have been manifesting extreme archetypal behaviour, as I did with 'rescuing' people, this is detracting from your attractiveness. You may also discover that when you allow the extreme characteristics to take over, you are attracting the wrong people into your life.

As you read through the list, you will become aware of which archetypes resonate with you. The work we are going to do later will help you to incorporate the positive qualities of your archetypes into your life.

As you read through the descriptions, do so with two thoughts in mind:

1. Where you recognize some of the negative extremes as part of your make-up, tick the box under the title 'Would like to transform'.
2. If you are drawn to some of the positive transformation qualities but know that this archetype is not part of your make-up, tick 'Would like a taste of''. Whilst some archetypes will be more predominant, a deeply attractive person has a mixture of all the positive archetypal qualities.

Once you come to terms with your archetypal tendencies, you can learn to harness their positive qualities and have them work for you rather than against you. Later I'll be offering you some ways to gain a taste of the other archetypal attributes and thus increase your universal attraction factors.

WHAT ARE YOUR ARCHETYPAL TENDENCIES?

Archetype	Negative extremes	Positive transformation	Would like to transform	Would like a taste of
Helpless baby	Craves approval, potential abusee, self-blaming, self-abusive, e.g., anorexia, needs protection.	Trusting, hopeful, loyal. Looks for the good in others.		
Orphan	Sense of abandonment, closed to offers of help, cynical, sense of unworthiness.	Able to accept help easily, integrating into groups, becoming inter-dependent.		
Victim	Blames others, shirks responsibility.	Aware of how easy it is to victimize others, alert to potential bullying.		
Superhuman	Must win, obsessive need for power, fears impotence, must appear strong.	Assertive, sense of vision, stands up for beliefs, attains goals.		

SECRETS OF ATTRACTION

Archetype	Negative extremes	Positive transformation	Would like to transform	Would like a taste of
Saviour	Fear of not being appreciated, over-protective, 'smother love', induces guilt, needs to be needed.	Guides and nurtures talent, cares for self in order to care for others. Able to empower.		
Adventurer	Obsessive need to be independent leading to loneliness, need for adrenalin rush, obsessive ambition.	Open to new ideas, experiments. Bold and daring. Seeks spiritual fulfilment.		
Saboteur/ Destroyer	Destroys good relationships, harms others, tramples on other people's feelings.	Able to break off relationships that are harmful. Lets go of damaging beliefs.		
Ruler/Monarch	Sense of own importance, superior to others, movie-star self-obsession.	Personal empowerment, wisdom, charismatic leadership.		
Lover/Artist	Obsessive love, jealousy, sexual addiction, envy.	Self-acceptance, finding life path. Passion and devotion, emotionally mature.		

Archetype	Negative extremes	Positive transformation	Would like to transform	Would like a taste of
Femme fatale/ Seducer	Plays with emotions, uses and dumps, dominates.	Great leader, inspirational, able to motivate, flirts for fun, not for gain.		
Creator	Obsessive, overdone. Dives in without thought, builds castles in the air. Workaholic, sets self up for failure.	Makes dreams come true, is into personal development, has a sense of destiny, spiritual maturity.		
Fool/Joker	Plays the fool to pacify others. Cries behind the painted smile. Self-mockery to cover lack of self-worth.	Able to laugh at self while maintaining self-esteem. Sense of humour about life, playfulness.		

Now that you have a sense of your archetypal make-up, think about those things you'd like to transform and ask yourself, for example:

'What would it be like to be more ... of a fool?'
'What would it take for me to become more ... creative?'

And if you don't know the answer yet, or how to go about developing the qualities you want, then stay with me. I'm here to help you find the answers you're looking for.

Robert was a manager in industry. He was responsible for 12 people. He believed that he was there to make decisions and that his team was there to put his decisions into action. He complained to me that they weren't pulling their weight. I showed him the archetypal table and asked him to pick the archetype which most fitted him at work. He chose 'Superhuman'.

Next I asked Roger to look down the list of positive transformation qualities and focus on that side of the Superhuman. How would it be to have a vision and to get his staff involved in developing goals that matched that vision? What would he have to do to nurture their talents?

Roger realized he would like to have more of the positive transformation qualities of the Saviour and also to transform from a dictatorial Monarch to a benign one. He agreed to pick a day when he was going to play the Saviour or the benign Monarch. On that day he would wake up and say to himself, 'Today is Saviour/benign Monarch day.' Then, when he was showering, commuting to work or doing anything else so commonplace that he would have plenty of time to let thoughts emerge, he was just going to say to himself, 'I wonder how I can empower, help and nurture my staff today?'

DISCOVER YOUR BE-SPOT

This has helped turn my life around and opened me to some truly powerful and exciting experiences.

What is a Be-spot? Everyone has one. It's also a Bliss-spot. It's the place where you have access to unlimited supplies of pure bliss. It's a pleasure button. It's a magic wand. It's the specific way your body is formed when you are in the zone, flowing, or whatever you call it. And you can learn to turn it on at will and live with the constant buzz of 'bliss' behind everything you do. And when you play with it you are at your unique best. When you turn up the force of your Be-spot, you are able to do anything you put your mind to. And, like that, you attract the people and situations that are perfect for you.

You have had those really good moments in your life haven't you? Those times when you were 'in the zone', 'flowing', 'happy', 'invincible', 'powerful' or whatever words you use to describe it. This is you drinking from the purest, deepest, most delicious wells of your Be-spot. You can have this bliss anywhere, anytime, in any situation, even when you're washing the dishes or in a 'boring' meeting. Once you learn how you 'do' bliss, and carry on doing it, it will become more and more natural to you. Your body language will change, your posture will shift and your face will appear softer. And you'll be sending out chemical messages that are irresistibly attractive to those people who are just right for you in every area of your life.

Stimulate your Be-spot

Stimulating your Be-spot is like indulging in a great new activity that does it for you sexually. Except this isn't about sex and you can play with your Be-spot all the time and in public, and the more you do it, the more other people are attracted to you. And the pleasure is more intense, more widespread and permeates your whole body with ripples of bliss!

STIMULATING YOUR BE-SPOT

Allow yourself a few moments to dwell on your dreamtime thoughts *(see page 52)*, relaxing now and sitting comfortably as you read this, noticing how your belly moves up and down when you breathe in and out. Imagine yourself living one of your attractive daydreams. Let it flow over you and give yourself up to it.

Before you read on, I suggest you read these explorations through to the end and then come back and do them at your leisure ...

Comfort Check

Find somewhere comfortable to sit. To help you get even more comfortable:

If your legs or ankles or arms are crossed, try uncrossing them.
Check your hands. Are they clenched or tight? If so, loosen them up.
Are your shoulders rounded? Maybe you need to pull them back and
    down just a little.
Is your spine straight or scrunched? Perhaps it would feel better if you
    stretched it a bit, just one vertebra at a time.

Does your head feel balanced on your shoulders? Try edging it back and forth bit by bit until it seems to sit in balance on your shoulders.

Notice the part of your body just beneath your navel. This is your *hara* point, your powerpoint centre. Focus on it.

As you breathe in and out, feel your belly expanding to let the air in and moving upwards and inwards to expel the air out again. Find your natural breathing rhythm.

- As you think about what bliss means to you, let your glance fall wherever it feels comfortable. Very, very slowly, let your eyes move around until your gaze seems to fall comfortably into one spot.
- Ask yourself, 'What's really true of me when I'm at my very best, when life seems perfect?'
- Answer *out loud:* 'When I'm at my best, I am [all your own wonderful qualities].'
- As you are saying this, notice how your body reacts. Maybe you nod your head or tap your feet or curl your toes or move your fingers or hands or breathe in a certain way ... We all do something. Become aware of how you do yourself at your best.
- When this begins to feel really good, you'll be tapping into your Be-spot.

Do this often.

Your Be-spot is more than a spot, it's your whole body and mind having a specific physical and mental experience of you at your best, and it's amazing, wonderful, awesome. You will have your own word for it. And you can have more of it. And it can help transform your life.

CREATING YOUR BLUEPRINT

You're beginning to get a sense of how you are at your best, when you are sparkling and resonating and feeling great. You are starting to understand that blueprint and maybe it's time to put it down on paper. Using words as symbols, you will create a blueprint for how you are at your best. Each word will come from you and will create specific feelings in you because of the associations it brings up. It's a fun game to play, and easy too.

YOUR 'DAZZLING WORDS' GAME

To play this game you will need some quiet time, a blank piece of paper, something to write with and, if you like colour, some coloured pens.

- Get comfortable in a place where it's easy to write. Then access your Bliss-spot. How are you when you are at your best? What's that like in your body? Where do you look? What do you feel? Enjoy it for a moment or two.
- Ask yourself what words sum up how you want to be. They may be words you found when doing the archetype exploration or they may be new words. Here are some to give you an idea ... or three:

dazzling	independent	active	vibrant
creative	graceful	powerful	vulnerable
generous	intense	resilient	open
understanding	alert	devoted	honest
funny	caring	effective	energetic
elegant	strong	concise	
imaginative	healthy	sharing	
resourceful	radiant	directed	

- Now allow your *own* words to come up and notice what's happening in your body as you do so. Focus on your heart area and feel a sense of love. It will generate some love-ly words ... All the words you come up with are important symbols for you.
- Write down your words as they come up. Let the stream flow.
- When you have finished, if there are any negative words, put them aside for the moment and focus on the other words.
- Look at each word. What does that conjure up for you? What do you see in your mind's eye? What sounds do you hear? Where are the feelings in your body and what are they like? If they are particularly nice, spend time basking in them ...
- Notice which words inspire you.
- Draw out your words, or type them up on the computer and enlarge them or embellish them and stick them up where you can see them. Make them beautiful, attractive, sexy, alluring and hot. These words are the symbols of your very own attraction template. More on this later.

THE LIVE-A-WORD-A-DAY GAME

Take as many days as you have words and have some fun playing the live-a-word-a-day game.

- Each day play with a new word.
- Before you go to sleep or as soon as you wake up, pick a word, for example 'open', and decide that today you will focus on being more 'open'. Say to yourself: 'Today I am being more open.'
- During the day, whenever you catch yourself being open (look out for nice feelings, they're a sure sign you're doing something right), smile to yourself or make a victory sign or say 'yes' or move around in some way. Congratulate yourself!
- Also be on the lookout for the quality in other people. Say to yourself, 'Today I'm going to become aware of when people are being open.' Notice how they move and talk when they are open. Also notice the feelings you get when you are in their presence. When you spend time with people who have the qualities that are emerging in you, it will help intensify those qualities in you.

> If you admire successful people, you create a positive force field
> of attraction that draws you toward becoming more and more
> like the kinds of people that you want to be like.
>
> **Brian Tracy**

- Most of all, spend time re-embodying and re-experiencing your words. They are a gateway to experiencing the great feelings you get when you are at your best.

And as you think about yourself at your best, you can also become aware of tuning in to the big wide world ...

TUNING IN ...

Tuning in to the World

Attraction only exists in the context of the world. If you were the only being on Earth, being attractive would be a useless attribute because there would be no one to attract! As it is, you are one of the members of a community, neighbourhood, organization, religion, family, race, gender, age, social or political group and a whole load more. You are part of the world. Every day you are out in that world in some form or another and even if you are at home alone, you're still part of it all.

Each of us feels this connection to the world in a different way:

Margaret said that when walking along the cliffs in South Wales she'd look down on the sea and realize she was part of something pretty awesome and would stop and just absorb it. She described it as 'feeling at one with nature'.

■ ■ ■

Pat told me that he felt it very strongly when he sang in public. He played in an Irish band at a local bar and people would come up to him and ask him to play their favourite songs. He said it was so special when he looked out and saw how much people were enjoying his work.

■ ■ ■

Steve said that when he went to a football game, he'd sometimes get overwhelming feelings of power being part of an excited crowd all cheering for the same team.

Although we might feel it more in certain circumstances, it's possible to be aware of this connection anywhere. Imagine what it would be like in a busy train. Instead of mentally cursing the people who were jammed in so closely to you, you would just feel empathy with them. Imagine smiling at everyone in the carriage, imagine the positive effect on them ...

When you are out in the world, do you have a positive effect on people, even in a small way? Today I was talking to one of the customer service agents at my credit card company. I had called to sort out an error and was in the middle of running through what I wanted, a bit briskly, when I noticed the agent starting to say in a not-so-friendly voice tone, 'Well, you signed for that in your contract ...' I thought, 'I can change this interaction.' I softened my voice and asked him if he got a lot of people shouting at him. Immediately his voice went down and I could feel the connection forming. The whole experience shifted for both of us. We had a great conversation during which he told me how he'd been a bit surprised once to find himself shouting at *his* bank manager. Suddenly I thought how awful it would be if I shouted at someone and that contributed a build up of frustration which made them more likely to shout at someone else ... and so on.

Every time you interact with someone else, you have the power to affect the way they feel. You can incite any emotion, from anger through to joy. When you use this power for the good of others, you become deeply attractive. I'm not talking Mother Teresa here, I'm suggesting that in everyday ways, with sometimes small gestures, you can make a *huge* difference to others.

Try it in any challenging situation. Instead of cursing someone, even if they've made a mistake, realize that there could be any amount of heavy stuff going on for them and forgive them. Then send them a nice thought.

Sparks will fly, attraction will kick in and your AQ will soar.

Tuning in to Yourself

You are a very important person. You know you can have a powerful effect on others. And most of the messages you send out to others are transmitted unconsciously as a result of how you are feeling at the time. They come out in the way you move, the level of energy you exhibit, the tone of your voice, the look on your face and the way you hold yourself. If you're feeling down, you're likely to transmit that, but if you're feeling excitement, wonder, curiosity or any other uplifting emotion, that's what other people will get too. You can see why this makes you more attractive!

The following exploration will help you to tune in to your best self more of the time.

YOUR HIDDEN TREASURE

As before, read this through first then come back to do the exploration when you have time for some bliss.

Before we begin, are you sitting comfortably?

Quick Comfort Check

Uncross limbs.
Loosen hands.
Pull back shoulders.
Straighten spine.
Balance head.
Focus on power point.
Breathe soft belly.
Blissful gaze.

I believe that everyone has some magic inside them waiting to fly out and infect the rest of the world. It's as if you have a jewel deep in your heart, which over the years has become covered over. That jewel is who you really are, the person you were put on this Earth to grow into. This exploration will help you to access your own personal jewel.

- Choose a jewel that appeals to you. It might be a precious stone or a crystal or a metal or something else that is precious and symbolizes the perfect you. If it helps, visualize the colour, shape and size, and even the smell and taste.
- Imagine that it is located in the centre of your heart.
- Imagine that it holds the DNA code to that deeply attractive you – the you that's living your dreams, the you that's out in the world attracting wonderful situations and people into your life and the you that knows how wonderful it is to just be you and to shine as much as any jewel on this Earth.
- And the cool thing is that the most valued jewels have flaws. Except they're not flaws, they are individual quirks that make each jewel unique – and special. In the antique world, the most valuable item is 'the only one of its kind'.

- And when you are able to look deep into the heart of this jewel, it will reveal your life playing out as it should, both right now and way into the future.
- Focus on the jewel and all that it represents. Tune in to how you are when you are at your best.
- Consider these questions. Look for the possibilities.

What's great about you?
What's hiding inside and waiting to shine out?
What's it like when you feel just right? When you are experiencing pure joy, ecstasy, excitement, bliss, fulfilment ... You know the word you use and you know what it's like to experience it. Great, isn't it?
By the way, what *is* your word? Whatever word comes up is perfect for you. This word is very powerful. Each time you see or hear it, it will bring back the sensations of you at your best.
Like this, *what's possible for you?*

Triggers

Part of tuning in to yourself is getting to know how you generate feelings. We learned in the first chapter how certain triggers can bring back good or bad feelings. Now it's time to look at this in more detail.

We know that our thoughts and reactions to things determine our feelings. Just by thinking of something we can generate feelings. Try the following exploration.

THOUGHTS ... AND FEELINGS

- Think of someone you really don't like, someone you have allowed to annoy, bully or insult you.
- Notice what's going on in your body.
- Now think of someone you really love, someone you'd do anything for, someone who is there for you, someone who makes you *feel good*.
- Doesn't your body do that differently?

Do this often and you will become very aware of the physical sensation of pleasant and unpleasant feelings.

As I mentioned earlier, when you know you are sliding into a not very useful thought train you can stop it and chose to do something different. When this happens to me, I have noticed that I'm usually sitting in a certain position and looking in a specific direction when I'm joining that thought train. The following exploration will help you to pick up on your own patterns.

FINDING YOUR PATTERNS

- When you catch yourself in a not so useful thought train, what direction are you gazing in?
- How is your body positioned?
- Remember wishing for something and then not getting it.

> How desperate were you to get it?
> How worried were you that you wouldn't get it?
> What did you imagine would happen if you didn't get it?
> When you thought about it, how often did you really believe that you would get it?
> Had you prepared for the fact that you might not get it? If so, how did you do that?
> Do you remember visualizing getting it? Did you say things to yourself about it? Did you share your feelings with others and if so, how?
> If you made a picture in your mind, was it as if you were experiencing it from your own perspective or were you watching yourself from a distance? Was the picture moving? Was it in colour? Was sound attached?
> Did you say something like 'I'd love to get this but I bet I won't' or did you say something like 'This is for me' or 'I feel so right getting this'?
> What kind of voice did you use? Was it an unpleasant one or one that tempted you sweetly?
> What feelings did you get and where were they in your body?

Now you should have some pointers on what to adjust in the pattern next time.

Once you are aware of how your body changes according to your thoughts, your stance and your focus, you can use this to generate more magic moments. And each time you experience those magic moments, you will be accessing your Be-spot and your AQ will soar. Here are a few quick tips to help your AQ rise even further!

Quick Tips to Boost your Attraction Quotient
KNOW WHAT YOU REALLY WANT

When I asked Terry what he wanted more than anything else, he answered immediately, 'I want to be famous.' I asked him what that would give him. He grinned sheepishly as he said, 'I'd get laid more often.' I didn't let it rest there. 'And what would that give you?' 'I'd feel more *special.*' Terry doesn't need to be famous and while it's nice to get laid more often, what he really wanted was to feel special. He might become famous one day and he might have women flocking to him, but until he believes he is special, fame and women won't change his self-esteem one jot!

Tip

When you think of something you want, ask yourself, 'What will that give me?' Do this until you end up with a big word like 'happiness' or 'freedom' or even simply 'feeling special' …

FOCUS ON WHAT YOU WANT, NOT WHAT YOU DON'T WANT

Some people have a habit of focusing on what's wrong or what they want to escape. Make sure you are putting your focus on what you want. You don't realize it, but that thought plants itself in your mind and is literally changing the chemical composition of your body and sending out magnetic messages …

Shelley was a 54-year-old physically beautiful and financially successful woman. When her partner died, she joined an internet dating agency and went through a series of short-lived relationships. As a child she'd never had much affection or attention from her parents and as a result she'd become quite needy. And the longer she was alone, the more depressed she became. She regularly complained that she hated being single and didn't like being alone. Guess what? She was devoting most of her time generating energy around being single and being alone. *And* she was giving out an air of desperation to all the men she met. As a result she attracted men who only felt powerful by feeding her neediness and she frightened off those who didn't like needy women, and she got more lonely and was still single …

Tip

Become aware of the times you complain about things or expect things to turn out wrong. The more quickly you notice when you're focusing on what you don't want, the easier it will be to adjust your sights to focus on what is perfect for you.

Dream Richly

> The person who sends out positive thoughts activates the world around him positively and draws back to himself positive results.
>
> **Norman Vincent Peale**

When Mark split up from his wife, he spent some time being single. Then one day he was walking down the road in a pretty good mood and he started to think about meeting someone. He said to himself, 'Wouldn't it be great to meet someone local and someone who's like me.' That evening he went to a local wine bar and met Nic. He couldn't believe it – she was almost exactly what he'd been dreaming of, right down to her boyish body. And he had actually been passing within one road of her office when he had had that thought. They've been living together for five years now. Before buying their current flat, they made a list of all the things they wanted. They got it all, down to the ready-made organic garden, the closeness to the sea and much more.

Tip

When you wish for something, make it a full-bodied wish. Write it out, draw it or make rich images in your mind. Talk to yourself about it. Go into detail and enjoy it.

KNOW THAT WHATEVER HAPPENS IS PERFECT

'Trust' is the key word here. The way you expect things to turn out will determine how things will work out. Decide everything will be OK and prepare yourself to delete the negative thoughts and enhance the positive ones. Be on the lookout for benefits, whatever the situation.

Jan had started her own business after being made redundant, but after a good start everything had gone flat. So she applied for a new job similar to her old one. She had really liked her old job and was delighted that something similar had come up again.

Although she was a really strong candidate, she didn't get the job. When she heard the news, she called me because she was quite upset. I reminded her that it was all meant to be and that she could interpret it as a sign to give her business one more shot. She did, and now she's attracting more clients than she can cope with and has become aware of a desire to work with young people. Looking back, she said, 'Thank goodness I didn't get that job. I had no idea of what I now realize is possible for me.'

Jan got just what she needed: the opportunity to keep at it and create something that was far more tailored to her than the job she thought she wanted!

Nurture your Dreams

This last bit is important, so please consider what I have to say carefully.

Goal-setting has become very popular. You learn how to set a positive goal and to know what it will give you and when and where and with whom you want it. You check the effect it will have on others and then you take action. People have achieved great results by setting goals. But sometimes goal-setting can get in the way of achieving your dreams.

The trouble with traditional goal-setting is that it can be easy to get bogged down in planning every step and as a result you are narrowing down the ways in which your goal can come about. You can get hooked on the steps rather than letting the dream grow and work out in its own way.

Instead, when you focus on what's waiting for you out there, rather than on the steps, you get a real sense of how it feels. This trains your body into the shape of success. So, once you have a strong sense of what you want, stop worrying about it. A watched dream rarely grows. Just relax and I promise you you'll start finding yourself drawn towards places, activities, events and people that are in a position to help further your dream. It's a bit magical, but it works when you trust in the process.

As for what your dream might be ... Who knows? But once you access your power and sense your connection to the world, you will find yourself discovering a strong sense of purpose. Your very own purpose is out there waiting for you to discover it.

If you are ready to go in search of your unique destiny, please turn the page ...

THE LURE OF PURPOSE

If a man is called to be a street sweeper, he should sweep
streets even as Michelangelo painted, or Beethoven composed
music, or Shakespeare wrote poetry. He should sweep streets
so well that the host of heaven and earth will pause to say,
'Here lived a great street sweeper who did his job well.'

Martin Luther King, Jr

You may be destined to be a street sweeper or a freedom fighter or a rock star or
a parent. Whatever your fortune, the world's your oyster. And there's a unique
pearl waiting for you. I believe the purpose of all our lives is to embark on the
journey to find that pearl and to live the best life we possibly can.

My local paper ran a story about a lady who had swept the roads of my town
for 30 years and had been awarded a medal for her services. The next time
I saw her I stopped to talk. I wanted to know what she loved about the job.

She pointed down the street where she'd just been working and said, 'I look
back and know I've made those streets nicer for everyone and that feels
good.' As she talked about it, she straightened up and breathed more deeply
and a beautiful smile covered her face. At that moment, she seemed very
powerful.

In his book *The Mastery of Love*, Don Miguel Ruiz reminds us that each of us is born with the same power as any other person in the world and:

> The main difference between you and someone else is how you apply your power, what you create with your power.

Even as a street sweeper you can use your power to contribute something valuable to the world. You don't need to have a glamorous job or live in a fantastic apartment or have loads of money or that elusive 'perfect' look and body to be valuable. And, despite all the fairy stories we're fed from birth, having all those things doesn't always make you attractive either.

> Lucy called initially to ask about some personal coaching. I thought she would get a lot out of coming on a course. I told her how much fun it was and how people shifted so positively … and then she said, 'It sounds great, but I have a problem with groups. They'll all be giving me that look as if to say "What on Earth are *you* doing here?"' I asked, 'Are you by any chance quite pretty?' She was. But she didn't feel attractive inside. She was like a fancy box of chocolates with no choccies inside.

When you discover and follow your dreams you will become very attractive, because you will be glowing from the inside with deep fulfilment. Following your purpose is immensely attractive …

YOUR LIFE PURPOSE

How in tune are you with your life purpose? When people call me to book courses or coaching, I always ask them: 'What do you do?' And then I ask: 'Do you like it?' I'd say about 60 per cent of the people I speak to aren't happy in the work they've ended up doing. Sometimes they come to me because they think a relationship will sort them out and they end up realizing the relationship they need to develop is the relationship with what they really want, with their own true purpose.

Are you a work-slave or is work more like play? Answer the questions below as instinctively as you can.

1. **You're on holiday and meet some new people. They ask you, 'What do you do?' Are you more likely to:**

a) Light up at the thought of sharing something that's so special to you and makes you feel so good.

b) Think, 'I don't want to be talking about work, I'm on holiday.'

c) Cringe or brush it off because what you're doing is so not you.

2. **You are doing your particular work because:**

a) It's what you've always dreamed of doing or you feel it's so right for you or it brings you great fulfilment.

b) It's what your family thought would be best or it's a 'good career' or it's too well paid to give up and anyway it would be too difficult to change now because you've come so far.

c) It's better than being out of work or it pays the bills, but you don't enjoy it and you'd rather be doing something else.

If you got more 'b's and 'c's, then maybe that's a message to get back on track. Or maybe it's time for a change ...

Knowing What's Right

> You are your own compass.
>
> **Paul Bauer**

You may not be fulfilled by what you are doing but be wary of making changes simply because you don't know what you do want to do. How do you know what's right for you? Sometimes when we don't know whether something is for us, it's useful to sit back and pay attention to our feelings. That way we can start to develop an instinct about what makes our heart sing and what doesn't.

Lynda was a corporate trainer and enjoyed her work. She'd recently been asked to apply for her manager's job when she left. She'd had sleepless nights mulling over what to do and had asked me to help her find out whether she really wanted the job.

I invited her to imagine for a moment that she was doing the job. I suggested that she imagine it as if she were in it, not watching herself doing it. The reason for this is that when you're sensing something through your own eyes, the feelings are stronger. I asked:

'What would your surroundings be like?'
'What would you be doing?'
'What skills would you be using?'
'What is important to you and how does this job match up?'
'Is it really you?'
'What would you gain from this and what would you have to give up?'
'What are the downsides and the upsides?'

Lynda made a short list:

Upsides:

Fantastic increase in salary and upgraded car.
I'll still be doing some training.
It's a step up the corporate ladder.
I can move to a bigger house.

Downsides:

Long hours.
My potential manager is a cold fish.
Having to play politics.

I got Lynda to read out her list to me and asked her how she felt as she looked at each item. After she had run through both columns, she said to me, 'You know, the strongest feeling I got was a sense of being trapped ... The long hours and the political games that go on at that level would be a restriction on my personal freedom.'

Where are you right now? The next exploration should help you to get a more resonant focus on your work and whether it's right for you.

SECRETS OF ATTRACTION

- Sit quietly for a minute or two and think about your work. Then open your eyes and jot down on a piece of paper all the thoughts that come up. You can write down sentences or individual words. Do not censor yourself. The point of this exploration is to see what's lurking beneath the surface.
- Check your list and divide it into three categories: 'upsides', 'downsides' and 'interesting'.
- Look at what you have written in each category or read it out loud to yourself. Which statements give you very strong feelings? What insights are you getting? What is the message or significance, particularly if you have stuff in the 'interesting' column?
- Now you are going to use your list to look for answers. Before you begin, say to yourself, 'I have access to all the answers I need.' Saying this instructs your brain to look for those answers. Brains are like heat-seeking missiles. When you program them in one direction, they follow it.
- Read the first word or phrase, say it aloud or move around while thinking of it. Look at it and then look up and allow yourself to dream. Close your eyes and ask, 'What does this mean and how important is it?'
- Do the same with each word or statement.
  Which gives you the strongest feeling?
  Does it override all the others?
  Does it feel really uncomfortable or does it make your heart sing?
- Think about what your feelings are saying to you.

If you feel that the work you are doing is part of your life's purpose, then that's great. If you still have doubts or are wondering whether there's more, stick with me, we've only just started.

We might as well begin with where it all begins – with your unique blueprint.

Tracing your Blueprint

> One must have the adventurous daring to accept oneself as a
> bundle of possibilities and undertake the most interesting game
> in the world – making the most of one's best.
>
> **Harry Emerson Fosdick**

Remember your blueprint? Each of us has a unique design for the perfect way to live our life. Your blueprint takes into account all the genetic and physical traits and abilities you have been endowed with and your talents and leanings – your 'bundle of possibilities'.

For some people these possibilities are clear at an early age.

William grew up in a small town in the north of England. His family was poor, but someone recognized he had a talent and paid for him to take music lessons with one of the best teachers in the area. With his teacher's encouragement he won a scholarship to the Royal College of Music. There he met his wife, Joan, who was also a musician. They had two children. William went on to become musical director for Marlene Dietrich and many other famous stars. He was a prolific composer and wrote music all his life. And he was always available to help others and encourage them in their musical careers. He gave a performance of his music the night before he died at the age of 81.

William found his path early in life because he was lucky enough to meet a mentor to encourage him to follow his dreams. But some of us don't find our path until we've inadvertently stepped onto another one.

A friend of mine, Caroline, is the daughter of a doctor and the granddaughter of a doctor. Medicine is 'in the blood' – or so her father always said. Caroline, a reluctant but dutiful daughter, went to Oxford and studied medicine. But throughout her time at university, there was hardly a day when she didn't question what she was doing. She knew, deep down, that she had to stop.

Even though she'd climbed a fair way up the medical ladder, when she realized it was the wrong one, she took that leap and jumped back down to the ground. Some people make the mistake of thinking that it's their 'fate' to be where they are and then make all kinds of excuses about how they can't change now or how they've 'come too far to go back'. Caroline was bold – she said that if she didn't let go she'd feel trapped for the rest of her life. She explored a few career routes before she finally ended up on her true purpose path. She now runs courses helping people to find direction in their lives!

SECRETS OF ATTRACTION

For others, like me, it is a long struggle to find the path.

> I was very clever at school, but rebellious. The teachers hated me because naughty pupils are supposed to get their just desserts by failing exams and I didn't. I wanted to study psychology at college, but the school had me lined up to go to Oxford or Cambridge, where all the academically clever girls went. I rebelled, refused to do the exams and went to a regular college, doing my 'best' subject, English. It was not what I wanted to do. I left after a year and for more than 20 years I was wandering with no idea what I wanted to do. I loved people and I wanted to help them, but I thought you had to have a degree in psychology to do that sort of work. I drifted from job to job and from adventure to adventure and from frustration to despair and then I got my wake-up call.
>
> I picked up a book called *Wishcraft* in San Francisco in 1985 and realized that it was possible to live the life I loved. Finally I had hope. It took me quite a long time to realize all the possibilities my blueprint held, because first I had to let go of being angry, blaming the world for my lack of luck, envying other people's success and complaining that life wasn't fair. I've come a long way on my journey but I remind myself every day that I'm not done yet, I'm a work in progress. Yet look at me now – anything is possible! And it is for you too when you are being yourself and are 'on print'.

Even when you wander onto a seemingly wrong path and slip into a downward spiral, your real path will continue to prod and call you in many different ways. Suddenly an event or an idea or something someone says will spark open your mind and send you spiralling up towards the door of possibility. And once you step through that door, the world truly is your oyster and your pearl is there to be harvested.

I'm going to help you trace your blueprint. We'll be paying attention to the things that you take pleasure in, your innate talents and how you want to be in the world, and will slowly begin to build up a sense of what it will be like for you to step through the door to your unique possibilities.

> Visualize this thing you want. See it, feel it, believe in it. Make your mental blueprint and begin.
>
> **Robert Collier**

Your Ideal Qualities

Sometimes you are inspired by people who have the qualities you want to cultivate in your own life. You adopt them as a symbol of that quality and their presence encourages you to strive for higher standards. Think of them as your magic helpers.

What qualities would you like to have more of? Let the ideas come up. Here are a few to get you going.

'I would like to be more ...'

compassionate	tolerant	determined	optimistic
generous	passionate	peaceful	enthusiastic
humble	adventurous	mindful	

'I would like to be more able to ...'

be myself	pay attention to	laugh at myself	negotiate
connect with	detail	believe in	see both sides
people	organize	myself	be aware of the
connect people	lead	simplify things	big picture
follow through	be a peacemaker	mediate	
and complete	make people		
things	laugh		

You get the idea ... You've got loads of great qualities already, but there are lots more out there that you can acquire. Open yourself to possibilities.

MEETING YOUR MAGIC HELPERS

- Make a list of all the qualities you have and also jot down four qualities that you want more of. Just for now, stick with four. But you can do this exploration over and over, adding more each time!

- Use your attraction journal to help you develop more of the qualities you want. If, for example, you want to be more tolerant, peaceful, able to negotiate and creative, write these down as headings in your journal. Leave a few free pages in between each one.

- For each quality, think of four people who are rich in that particular quality. They don't have to be real, they can be cartoon characters or people you've made up, but pick people who really shine out in a particular area. If I were to choose someone to enhance my ability to create feelings with the spoken word, for example, I'd choose Martin Luther King.

- Imagine your magic helpers in all their vivid glory. And hear them speaking to you.

- What are they telling you about their quality? What advice are they giving you from their experience?

- How does it make you feel being in the presence of that quality? Imagine how you could make other people feel if you had it. You would be attractive to them, wouldn't you?

You can call your helpers up at any time and have them appear before you, just as you would call a genie by rubbing a magic lamp. All you have to do is call and they'll be there. And sometimes, when you really get the sense of a quality you want more of, you find yourself meeting real magic helpers who are there to teach you just what you need to learn.

Whether you use the magic helper concept or not, it's really beneficial to personalize how a quality will show up in you. After all, what you mean by creativity may be very different from what I mean by it.

- Under the heading for each quality, write out different ways in which you sense you are developing it, for example:

'I am becoming more tolerant when I don't allow other people to annoy or anger me.'

'I feel more peaceful when I am able to recognize my potential and stop criticizing myself.'

'I am able to negotiate better because I am developing a much better feel for what makes people tick and I am going for win-win solutions.'

'I am enhancing my creativity in writing by reading more and keeping a notebook of ideas.'

- Then you can record the consequences having more of that quality, for example:

  'When I am more tolerant, I am more relaxed and I find out things about people that surprise me.'

  'When I am more peaceful, I find myself getting some great ideas.'

  'When I negotiate better, I make the right deals and let go of the ones that aren't for me.'

  'When I am more creative, I get ideas, I see possibilities and I find solutions more easily.'

You are training your brain by letting it have a taster of what you want and also giving it some benefits to focus on. All you have to do is make up your mind to have more of the quality you want. The rest will follow.

Your Ideal Work

If you love what you do, you will never work another day in your life.

Confucius

LOVING WHAT YOU DO

■ Think for a moment of all the things you love doing. Jot them down. Here are a few ideas:

helping other people meet their needs	taking risks	growing things	researching information
fighting for a cause	putting your stamp on the world	designing things	solving mysteries
persuading people	being responsible for big deals or projects	creating things	analysing information
pleading a cause	initiating projects	coming up with creative solutions	generating theories
acting as a catalyst	selling ideas to others	developing new ideas	debating
motivating people	solving problems	making things beautiful	learning new things
nurturing people	negotiating	thinking creatively	working with intelligent people
teaching people	closing deals	performing	working with procedures and manuals
finding out about people	fixing things	leading	keeping accurate records
mentoring	putting things together	fighting for justice	organizing
counselling	making things	exploring	taking care of detail
leading	figuring out how things work	acting spontaneously	
healing	working with machines and tools	creating a vision	
advising		working with numbers and scientific data	
promoting			
selling			

At this stage we're not even going to try to translate this into a specific type of work. What we are going to do is lay the foundations for that to emerge naturally. Pinning a label on yourself too quickly stops you from dreaming fully so you miss out on the possibilities.

■ For now, look at your list and use it to inspire you. Because now you're going to make a list of statements about what you love doing. These declarations will serve as a reminder to keep on track.

- Go through each item on your list and say 'I love doing ...'
- Notice the ones that really grab you. These are the elements that you are going to use to construct your ideal day.

Your Ideal Day

Eighteen years ago, I did an exercise which required me to describe my ideal day. At the time the life I was living bore no resemblance to the day I imagined. But curiously, much of it has materialized

Here's what I wrote. As you read it, think of how much more descriptive it could have been.

> I wake up in my own white airy house somewhere where the sun shines a lot, near water. It's very peaceful. I take a swim for half an hour in my pool and then make some breakfast of freshly juiced fruit. I sit for half an hour or so outside with my partner and talk or read the paper or just drink in the warm glow of the sun and the sound of insects. Then I take a shower ...

> I'm doing a show tonight or I might be giving a workshop. I'm going over my notes. My secretary arrives and makes sure everything is OK. For the rest of the morning I'm working on my projects, preparing and researching, making contact with interesting people. I'm driving into town in my convertible, lunching with friends and interesting people, shopping at my leisure, preparing dinner for friends and spending time with my loved ones.

That dream of my ideal day reinforced my determination to find out what was waiting out there for me. I went off track a lot, because it took me a while to find people to learn from and to guide me. You are more fortunate, because I'm here to help you stay on the path.

Remember that during your ideal day you could receive an e-mail or a letter or meet someone who is a connection to something else that leads to *another* ideal day. Use your imagination – there are no limits.

MY IDEAL DAY

- Before you go to sleep, tell your brain to go on a search for lots of detail about your ideal surroundings and everything that's going on during your ideal day. Add in colours and full visual effects. You want to be able to get a real sense of a drop of water on the leaf of a tree or your name in print on a book or the faces of the people you are attracting. Ask for a soundtrack, some funky tastes and some juicy smells ... So, are you ready to step into your ideal day?
- Imagine tomorrow morning. You wake up and find that you are engaged in your ideal life's work. What you are doing is bringing you utter bliss in many ways, despite the ups and downs. What are you doing and what does it feel like?
- Look, listen and feel. Use all your senses to pick up the details.

> **Where are you living and working? Describe your surroundings in as much detail as you want. What country are you in? What items are around you as you work? How do they benefit you during your ideal day?**
>
> **Who is in your life and how do they fit into your ideal day? What do they look like? What kind of character do they have? What is their role?**
>
> **What are you looking forward to? What is happening that will bear fruit later? What phone calls or chance meetings are occurring that will connect you to another ideal day?**

- Just be aware of the images and sounds and feelings that come to you. You can include anything from your current life and add in all the new things you want to.
- And when the ideas come up, write them down or say them out loud or make a tape or draw a picture, whichever method suits you best. Start with 'I wake up and ...' Write in the present tense. That makes it feel more real.
- When you have finished, read it through and allow it to sink in.

Keep this material somewhere you can access it regularly. If you wish to add to it or change it, great, that means you're getting even more focused on what you really want.

Would you like to believe it's possible? It is, with a little help from your friends.

Your Ideal People

We attract people into our lives because they are right for us at that time. As we change, we attract people accordingly. As we become more attractive, what kind of people do you think we attract?!

Every working situation involves some kind of interaction with people, either colleagues, clients or managers or someone we communicate with during the day. These people will reflect the quality of your day. The more you are doing the things you love, the more you will attract the kind of people who foster your growth and make you more attractive.

Think for a moment about the following questions:

What kind of people do you truly want in your life?
If you work in an organization, what sort of people do you want around you on a daily basis?
If you have clients or customers, what kind of people do you want to attract?
What qualities would these people have and how would that benefit you?
Why would they be attracted to you? What could *you* offer *them?*

Mary ran a garden design business from a shopfront office in a small parade of shops. She was highly creative, but rather disorganized and indecisive. And so were her clients. She would give them loads of suggestions and ideas, but most of them would ask for time to think about them and then not get back to her. When she wasn't visiting clients, Mary worked on her own. She wanted a public window for her designs, but being in the shop made her feel lonely. She wanted to attract customers who would be inspired by her ideas and hire her on the spot, and she wanted to have quality relationships with other people in her work environment.

Mary realized that she would have to bring some order into her own life and be more decisive about what she wanted. She put her design ideas on a website and moved her base to a creative business centre where she shared facilities with a graphic artist, a lifecoach and an osteopath.

Now Mary is set up to attract a different kind of customer because she is generating a different kind of attitude to her work and being with creative people will spark off new ideas in her.

As you step into your purpose, you will find people just turning up in your life at the very moment you need them. And they can help you on your heroic journey.

Your Heroic Journey

> Purpose, does not usually appear as a clearly framed goal, but more likely as a troubling, unclear urge coupled with a sense of indubitable importance.
>
> **James Hillman, *The Soul's Code***

Why do films grab us and draw us in? What is the secret of their allure?

The fact is that most box-office hits are based on the mythical hero's journey. This phrase was coined by Joseph Campbell, whose lifework was the study and unravelling of mythology. He discovered that there is a structure to the way we lead our lives and that structure is present in stories across every culture, past and present, throughout the world.

Most people would agree that life is a journey. Some think that we have no control over it while others think they have the power to shape their destiny ...

Here's how the heroic journey works:

- You are living a life and it might be a life that someone else set up for you. You may have gone to college because someone else wanted you to. Maybe you got married because that was what everyone did. Whatever set you on your path, if it's not your true path you will begin to get messages. You will feel dissatisfied in some way. It might be a nagging doubt or what my friend Pat called 'a tiny but constant knot in my stomach'. And if you ignore the call and carry on because it's too scary to contemplate what it might set off, it just gets even *louder*.
- And then one day, for whatever reason, you begin to think, 'Maybe there *is* something else.' And during this time, someone or something comes into contact with you. It may be someone you meet by chance or a book you suddenly notice. It can be anything. But it plays a significant part in your taking the first step.

- And then you decide 'Oh, why not, let's go for it!' You don't know what will happen, you're scared but you're excited at the same time. You trust that it will work out – and you make some plans too!
- And then you will meet people who try to put you off. They raise all kinds of reasons why you shouldn't change and emphasize what you have to lose. Sometimes they wear you down almost to the point of giving up. Beware, because they are there to test the strength of your resolution. When you know something is for you, even if you're really scared, you are prepared to take the leap.
- And when you take that leap, surprise surprise, all sorts of things start to appear – people, circumstances, opportunities, all conspiring to help you on your way.
- And sometimes the journey gets rocky, and it can be a bit of an ordeal and the going is tough. But the more you're locked into your destiny, the more strength you find to continue. Somehow you get through, with a little help from your friends and from the universe.
- And then you are living your life in a new way with all the benefits of the experience and the results of your taking that leap into the dark night of possibility. Life seems so much more alluring – as do you! And then you get the next call to adventure …

Your Purpose Star

Twinkle, twinkle, little star.
How I wonder what you are
Up above the world so high,
Shining brightly in the sky.

Relax, you don't have to wonder any more. The star that's been twinkling in the sky all these years is your purpose star. You can't always see it because sometimes there are clouds in the way. These are your clouds. They are holding you back from reaching for your star. But take heart, there is a way to break through.

The more you begin to think of yourself at your best, the more you're drawn to your purpose star. The two seem magnetically attracted to each other. You already have some sense of how it is when you are tuned in to who you are. You know how nice it is when you've massaged your Be-spot and set off a chain reaction of pleasure. You know you are connected in so many ways to so many people, things and places. You are aware that there is no one else like you on this Earth and that you can shine in your own unique way. And like that, *anything is possible.*

Your body has memorized a precise structure for how you are at your best, and you can help your brain to recognize it. You can begin to make a 'body map' of how you are when you lock on to your star.

LOCKING ON TO YOUR PURPOSE STAR

Take a moment or two to sit quietly and read this exploration through before you do it. If you can, tape the words and play them back to yourself.

This exploration works by commanding your brain to search for what it already knows and to make that known to you.

First do the quick comfort check:

Uncross limbs.
Loosen hands.
Pull back shoulders.
Straighten spine.
Balance head.
Focus on power point.
Breathe soft belly.
Blissful gaze.

- Take a moment or two to get a sense of connection to the world. Sometimes this sense of connection has a very peaceful, almost meditative feel to it. It is not a place where things happen. But it is a place where you can get inspiration to act in line with your purpose. That's what you're going to do now.
- Once you have your sense of connection, think about the feelings and body posture this generates in you. Think about what's special about you, what makes you the only one of your kind in the entire world.
- Now access your Be-spot and tune in to your bliss.

- Now move between the two, feeling your sense of connection to the world and then feeling how you are at your best.
- As you continue to do this, they will begin to blur into one ... and somewhere in the middle lies your purpose star. Somehow you will get a sense of it, a sense of your purpose. Even if it is just a fleeting undefined feeling, your brain will lock onto it and will recognize it again.

You can do this exercise as often as you wish and wherever you want. It will help you to recognize when you are acting out your purpose in the world.

LIFE HAPPENS. WHAT'S NEXT?

> It's a big mistake to dwell on what went wrong. The only way forward, when life comes up, is to keep focused on your purpose and ask relentlessly, 'What's next?' Spend your energies on moving forward towards answers and solutions. Ask yourself how you can turn this around.
>
> **Denis Waitley**

Living your life is like sailing the ocean. You will sail into storms, high winds and rain, but you also sail into sunshine, calm seas and beautiful lagoons. Living life at your best doesn't mean you won't hit the storms, because you will. But you'll learn to avoid most of them. And when you do encounter storms, it's a chance to become more skilled at the game of life. No matter what the circumstances, ask, 'What can I learn here?' and then direct your focus towards possibility and hope. Attractive people do not wallow in their problems. They know that ups and downs are part of life and that tomorrow something better will come along.

As I was writing this chapter, a series of stormy waters rocked my boat. What happened to me – or rather, what I generated in my life! – might give you food for thought and open up some possibilities. Here's how I sailed through one particular storm and ended up in the lagoon.

Two weeks ago I had a car and motorbike accident within two days of one another. The damage to the bike wasn't covered by the insurance and I didn't know whether I'd get enough from the car insurance to buy a similar quality car. I was bruised and battered, I had a book to write and in 10 days I was flying abroad to film a week-long TV show. The next day my shower packed up.

All these events coming on top of each other had the potential to be very traumatic if I had chosen to view them that way. Worries did zap into my mind about the inconvenience of not having a car and about losing my beloved scooter. But I recognized the beginnings of not so pleasant feelings in my body and said to myself, 'Downward spiral alert. Time for action!' Remember that when you are on the lookout for these downward spirals you can *stop* and direct your thoughts in another direction, literally. And when you choose to do this, all kinds of possibilities come up.

> Every adversity, every failure, every heartache carries with it the seed of an equal or greater benefit.
>
> **Napoleon Hill**

I started by telling myself, 'OK this is happening for a reason. *What's the lesson here?'*

Almost immediately, I had the answer: 'Slow down.' This warning was strong enough to make me stop and do something about it. I cancelled speaking at a conference and decided to use the two days to chill and write when I felt like it.

I also realized I had to take some time to get some urgent things done which had been weighing on my mind. I had to see the doctor for a check-up before I went away, I had to process my insurance claim and I had to sign a mortgage application form. Once these were done, I would create a smoother flow for myself.

And then I did some chi kung which calmed me and balanced my energy. I focused on my purpose – which is to open doors and to lead people to their own juicy delights! – and I put on Madonna's *Ray of Light* and started to write.

And the next day I sailed into a beautiful calm blue lagoon and fascinating things happened:

A TV company which was going to film me that week called to say they wanted to postpone.

My impending Scottish seminar was moved to later in the year.

**An old friend called out of the blue and helped me with my insurance claim.
I got the chance to purchase a great car for a lot less than it was worth. It's
perfect for what I need.**

I felt as if I were floating on my back in the lagoon and I reflected on the storms
I'd come through and all the good things that came out of the experience …
Even so-called 'iffy' experiences always have a hidden treasure.

If you are in a storm right now, here are a few hints on how to get to the lagoon:

- *Make a choice.* Things happen. When you choose to remain calm and rise
  above the situation, you distance yourself from your emotions.
- *Inject possibilities.* Once you accept that everything happens for a reason,
  you can move forwards and look for the lessons and solutions. It's useful to
  realize that change plays a valuable role in our life. Sometimes when you
  lose things, it means that a space is opening up for something that's more
  right for you. And sometimes when you don't get something it means
  there's something better round the corner.
- *Look for meaning.* Ask yourself: 'What's the lesson here?' Listen to your
  own messages.
- *Take action.* Connect with your purpose and work out what you need to do
  next. If you can't fix something, move on. If you can, carry out damage
  limitation and then you'll be freer to focus on the bigger purpose.
- *Let go.* Trust the system to take care of itself. It will. Let the tide carry you
  away to the blue lagoon and trust that it will all work out perfectly. And it
  will – if you believe that whatever happens is part of the perfect plan for you!
- *Find the hidden treasure.* And then sail into the lagoon to await your next
  adventure!

A LAST WORD

What's it like to have a good sense of who you are, what you are good at, what you
want and what's right for you? Pretty amazing, eh? But we've not finished yet.

It's time to charge up your energetic attraction. Turn the page and let's get
energized …

CHAPTER 5

ENTICING ENERGY

When energy is dancing in you, in unison, in deep harmony, in
rhythm and flow, you become a blessing to the world.

Osho

In previous chapters we've focused on setting free your attractive inner self.
And as you develop your inner self, your outer self will reflect those changes.
Your body will display your good inner feelings in improved posture, more
relaxed breathing and a lack of muscular tension. Pretty attractive, eh?

And it works the other way round too. As you work on loosening up and
aligning your body, you'll feel the effect on the inside. When you do both, you
get a double-whammy feel-good effect!

In this chapter I'll be using various tried and tested bodywork methods to
help you get a feel for how your body is affected by your emotions so that you
can do what feels better. And I'll be giving you a taster of body-management
techniques which can really help to release tension and cultivate physical
balance. And, if you're so inclined, you can dip your toes into the power of
tantra, which will help you express your sexuality.

With your body and mind working in harmony, as they were designed to,
you will be even more alluring!

BODYTALK

What is bodytalk? Most of us associate 'body language' with specific movements meaning specific things. But I want you to think instead about how your own body talks first to you and then to the outside world. That way, you can develop your own best body language and have the skill to read other people without having to make judgements.

We all respond to others in terms of what their body says. We make decisions about whether we like or trust them, what their mood is and even the way they approach life. We size up how sexy, attractive, alive and strong they are. And while we're doing that, they're doing it to us!

Bodywords

We give away clues to our emotions by the way we refer to the body in our *spoken* language. Our language is rich in 'bodywords'. Being aware of these words and how we use them helps us to get in touch with our body as a living, expressive, changing entity.

As you read through the following list of phrases, focus your mind on the parts of the body that are mentioned and notice what thoughts and sensations come up for you.

The Face

- *On the face of it.* Think about your face and the faces of people you know. We often use the word 'face' to speak about the outward appearance of things. This suggests that although the face is the first place we look when we are interacting with someone, we are aware that there is more.
- *Putting on a brave face.* How often do you put on a brave face? What other kinds of face do you put on? When we put on faces, we are hiding our true feelings behind a mask. This fools very few people, although many people choose to accept things 'at face value'.
- *Losing face.* This is a term we use to denote a blow to our self-esteem. When you lose face, your face literally drops and acts out a flood of emotions. You are no longer 'putting on a face'. What would happen if you were strong enough to 'face up to things' instead?

- *Keep your chin up.* We say this to encourage people, to boost their spirits when times are hard. When the chin drops and quivers it's often a sign that someone is about to cry.
- *If looks could kill.* We can manipulate our face so that it sends out a flood of nasty emotions to someone. Often we do it unconsciously! What kind of looks do you send out? What might you achieve by monitoring how your feelings are affecting your looks and making a conscious effort to send out loving looks more often?

The Neck and Shoulders

- *Sticking your neck out.* When someone sticks their neck out they are moving forward and exposing their face. It is both vulnerable and powerful. It is taking a risk. How often do you take risks and what do you lose by not sticking out your neck sometimes? Is your neck held stiffly in your shoulders?
- *Shouldering responsibility.* If your shoulders slump forwards it might be because you have too much going on in your life and it's overwhelming you. If they are tense, maybe you're trying too hard to hold back the tide.
- *Swallowing your words.* How often do you swallow your words? When you feel a lump in your throat, you are literally being choked by words unsaid or emotions unexpressed.

The Heart

Our language is full of expressions involving the word 'heart'. We think of our heart as the core of our being.

- *My heart sank.* We get feelings in our heart when we are confronted by severe disappointment or anxiety.
- *My heart isn't in it.* When this is the case you are doing something that isn't in harmony with who you are. Notice when your heart isn't in things and how that affects you. Maybe the feeling is telling you to place your heart somewhere else, where it can beat more freely.
- *My heart is broken.* This is the sense of your heart being cut off from the world when you have been hurt.
- *To lose your heart.* When someone falls in love they often feel as if they no longer have control over their heart because someone else has it.

■ *To open your heart.* Attractive people have the ability to open their heart to send and receive love freely. This is one of the most powerful qualities you can develop.

To become more aware of your body and how it talks, start by noticing bodywords when they come into a conversation.

While we are busy using bodywords, our body is equally busy shaping itself in relation to our emotions. Learning to understand how your emotions affect your body is vital if you are to realign yourself in order to move and interact in a more attractive way.

Bodyenergy

Many respected forms of therapy are based on the theory that your body is a map of your emotions. Bioenergetics is one such therapy and I have drawn heavily on it in this section because it makes complete sense to me.

Alexander Lowen, one of the creators of bioenergetics, says: 'Bioenergetics is a therapeutic technique to help a person get back together with his body and to help him enjoy, to the fullest degree possible, the life of the body.' We might not need actual therapy (yet!) , but we can still learn from the model.

Do you remember being told as a kid not to make faces because the wind would change and you'd get stuck like that? That wasn't an old wives' tale, it was the truth. We do get stuck in certain unattractive postures on a regular basis. Have you ever had the experience of watching TV or a film and realizing you've been frowning for a long time? There are plenty of other looks and postures that are equally unattractive. If you start by being aware of what you're putting out there, you can begin to change it.

Your body is like a museum of all your past emotions. As a baby your body was loose, vulnerable, open, relaxed, ready for action, very mobile and able to reach out in all directions. Energy flowed naturally and you had a gentle pulse or rhythm that was regular and easy.

As you came into contact with the world, this naturally flowing energy made contact with other kinds of energy. When I talk about 'energy' I mean different situations and other people's negative and positive emotions. Whenever we encounter a strong form of energy there's a rude interruption of the natural flow and rhythm of our bodies. When your 'heart skips a beat' that's an expression of what actually happens when you experience certain emotions

– your heart beats irregularly. When something 'takes your breath away' it means that for a moment you stop breathing or take in or let out a massive stream of breath. The natural flow of your breathing is interrupted.

When we come into contact with things that feel good, we open up to them inside and out. Our posture expands and our limbs separate and we smile. When we come into contact with unpleasant emotions, we literally contract. Muscles clench, breath is held and the body tenses up. We arm ourselves to resist.

> Robert was a hyperactive child. He was constantly told to stop fidgeting. As a result, when he felt the urge to fidget he remembered his mother's disapproving shout and anger and he clenched his fists and held his arms very rigidly at his side. His body developed the habit so much that he spent most of him life clenching his fists and holding himself rigidly. He appeared stiff and lifeless. His inner glow was so restricted by his body that he couldn't let it out.

When we contract it's as if we're building a defence against our true feelings. Our rhythms become discordant and we start to bend and twist into unpleasant shapes. And we don't look attractive.

> Genevieve worried constantly about what people would say about her. One day we were standing by the window looking down at the view, or so I thought, when Genevieve's hand shot out to straighten the net curtain. As she did so she started to mutter, 'They're really critical round here – they pick up on everything.' And then I noticed that her back had begun to curve and quite unconsciously she had stopped speaking out loud but was just moving her lips. And the more she muttered, the more her back bent over. I stopped her and pointed it out. She was horrified to realize that she was creating a dowager's hump for herself. Not a pleasant thought at 32, but a useful one. Once you are aware of what you are doing, you can do something else.

As you begin to work on the bits of your body that are stuck, you will also find yourself releasing the link to the emotions that made you get like that in the first place. And as you do that, you are freeing up your body to learn what it is like to be joyful, alive, lissom, sensual and expansive.

Sometimes just thinking about what that would be like is enough to shift your body. So what's it like when your body is aligned and flowing? Why not try it out for yourself with the following exploration?

EXPERIENCING THE FLOW

- Stand up (or, if you can't right now, sit up) and keep your feet apart with your buttocks loose and unclenched. Feel your feet firmly planted on the ground and keep your head balanced on the top of your neck. Imagine you have a golden string at the top of your head that draws you upwards. Let your shoulders droop and your arms hang down.
- As you breathe in, feel your chest rising upwards. Begin to rock and sway from your hips. Lift your arms to your side and stretch them as far as you can. Move your shoulders back and forth in circles and purse your lips in a sexy kissing motion as you do so, finishing by licking your lips and smiling.

I bet that feels nice, doesn't it? That's just a tiny taster of how it feels when you let your body go and experience the flow.

ANCIENT ARTS OF BODY MANAGEMENT

Have you noticed how some people seem to have the wonderful ability to remain calm, relaxed and balanced? These are qualities I realized I needed more of in my life and a large number of my clients did too. Many of my clients are busy people with high-powered jobs. They come to me because they've been so focused on climbing the corporate ladder they've let their life get out of control. They've not taken time to chill out (a furious session at the gym is *not* what I mean by chilling out!), enjoy life and build satisfying relationships. They need calm and balance. I often recommend they take up the ancient arts of yoga and chi kung.

Yoga and chi kung are based on a sense of connection to the world, balance, breathing and the belief that the mind and body are interconnected and that a combination of movement, positive thinking and breathing can ensure our energy is used in the best possible way.

I first studied yoga at the Sivananda Vedanta Yoga Centre in London. The teachers lived on the premises, wore simple white cotton clothing, spoke softly and glided as they walked. The first time I crossed the threshold, I sensed a warm calm energy which gave me a feeling of deep relaxation. It was like being transported to another world.

I had a very similar experience when I started chi kung with my teacher Peter Hudson. We were in a bare church hall, but once we started the class all I noticed was energy building in me and a growing connection with the other people there. Peter talked gently to us, focusing our minds on the spiritual aspect of the movements we were making. It was like swimming in calm waters. Afterwards I felt energized, uplifted and really serene.

What a contrast to our modern working life where we rush around, criticizing and blaming each other, getting impatient with each other, not taking time to listen, worrying about what was and what might be, competing and pushing ourselves too far. These are the symptoms of a modern dis-ease. When we behave like this our body generates a negative concoction of fight-or-flight chemicals, our body language reflects what's going on inside (not pleasant!) and people pick up these stressful and unpleasant signals. Like this, *no one* is attractive.

Luckily, the very first time you take a class in either of these ancient arts, you will discover easy techniques to instantly reduce stress. A simple breathing exercise or stretch or movement is sometimes all it takes to radically shift the way you feel.

Breathing: Your Life Force

Breathing keeps you alive, but good breathing refreshes and inspires you. Both yoga and chi kung are grounded firmly in correct breathing. Fundamental to yoga is the movement of *prana*. *Prana* is the life force that is carried in the air, food water and sunlight. Yogic breathing is designed to facilitate its passage around your body.

Think about this idea for a moment. What is it like to believe that you can enhance your life force by breathing properly?

When I first started yoga, I was bowled over by the fact that I'd been breathing the wrong way for most of my life. Most of us breathe very shallowly and we tend to feel our chest moving inwards as we breathe in and outwards as we breathe out. This is absolutely not what our body wants to do!

This simple breathing exercise is designed to help you breathe the way your body really wants to.

BELLY BREATHING

- Lie down with your arms by your sides, palms facing upwards and your legs a little apart. Notice where your body touches the ground and where you are supported. Imagine the earth is supporting your whole body. Start with the heels and the back of the legs and let them sink into the floor. Then work your way upwards to your thighs, your buttocks, your shoulders and the back of your head. Imagine that you are a sack of potatoes that has been dropped to the floor, and just flop.
- Keep your tongue in contact with the roof of your mouth just at the back of your front teeth. (This allows the energy you breathe in to circulate throughout your nervous system without a break.)
- Place your attention on your belly, about two or three inches below your belly button. Begin to breathe in. As you do so, you should notice that your belly is expanding outwards and downwards and is getting fuller. Notice how your chest seems to expand outwards, sideways and downwards, as if the air is filling both chest and belly.
- As you breathe out, notice how your belly goes flatter and your chest area seems to shrink slightly as the air moves up through your chest and out of your mouth or nose.
- Imagine you are breathing from that point below your belly button and feel the breath come all the way in. Notice how your spine feels, as if it's extending from that mid point both upwards and downwards as your shoulders come down. What's actually happening is that you're using a muscle called the diaphragm, which is located directly under your lungs. When you breathe in, your diaphragm moves away from your lungs and belly, allowing the lungs to expand and take in the air. When you breathe out, the diaphragm moves in again to force the air out.
- Focus your attention on your breath coming in and out. If your mind starts to chatter (the Chinese call this the 'monkey mind'), just acknowledge your thoughts, imagine them leaving as you breathe out and bring your attention back to your belly and your breathing.

- As you breathe in, imagine yourself being filled with lovely golden sparkly energy, and as you breathe out, imagine all the nasty stuff leaving via your mouth and also going down through your legs into the ground.

Practise this breathing every day. Gradually build up the time until you can do five, then ten then fifteen minutes. Then put it into action during the day. It's a powerful way to still your mind, release worry and allow all those wonderful positive attractive thoughts to surface.

Now let's look at these ancient body-management arts in more detail.

Yoga

You're probably familiar with yoga even if you haven't tried it. But you might not be so familiar with the principles and purpose of it. The word *yoga* means 'joining'. The aim of yoga is to align yourself with your body and to harmonize with the world – just like the stuff we've been doing in the last two chapters! Millions of people all over the world have been practising yoga for years and gaining huge value from it. And you can too.

Yoga is based on five principles and when you consider them they make perfect sense:

1. *Positive thinking and meditation* help remove negative thoughts and still the mind.
2. *Relaxation* reduces muscle tension, conserves energy and releases fear.
3. *Exercise* works systematically on all parts of the body to keep the spine flexible and improve circulation.
4. *Breathing* makes use of the entire lung area to increase the intake of oxygen and helps to recharge the body and mind by regulating the flow of energy.
5. *Proper diet:* A well-balanced and nourishing diet based on certain foods keeps the body light and the mood upbeat.

RELAXATION AND BREATHING

The physical side of yoga consists of stretching movements and breathing exercises. The breathing calms your mind, focuses your energy and enhances your movement. The stretching stimulates your internal organs, expands your muscles and allows your lifeblood to flow more freely through your body.

As children we delight in exercising every muscle. This natural activity keeps our body balanced. As we grow up we often do repetitive tasks where we are in one position for too long. For example, I sit at my desk typing for long periods and often find myself falling into bad posture habits. If you're like me, then you need this next exercise too.

RELEASING TENSION

This simple 10-minute process will really help stretch out your body and release any areas of tension. It's nice to do before you go to bed at night or when you wake up.

- Lie on your back with your arms out to your side, palms up, a little away from the sides of your body. Your legs should be open to about hip width.
- Stretch your neck and pull your chin in.
- Feel your belly fill up and relax as you breathe in and out.
- Start with your feet and legs. Lift your leg an inch off the floor, tense it from the foot up to the thighs and then let go and drop it back to the ground. Repeat with the other leg
- Clench your buttocks together; lift your hips a little off the floor and hold. Relax and drop them to the ground.
- Raise your arm an inch from the floor, clench your fist and tense your arm muscles, then let it drop. Repeat with the other arm.
- Tense and raise your chest and back off the floor, relax and drop back down.
- Hunch your shoulders tight up against your neck and then let go.
- Squeeze all the muscles in your face towards your nose then smile and let go.
- Keep your eyes closed and stick out your tongue as far as it will go. Relax and stick it back in again.
- Tuck your chin in slightly and roll your head gently from side to side until you find the point of balance and relax.
- Visualize your body and say to yourself, 'I relax my toes, I relax my calves,' etc., covering every part of your body from tippy toe to the top of your head.

- As you breathe in, feel a wave of oxygen going down to your feet, and as you breathe out, feel the tension flowing out of your body.

COUNTERBALANCE AND STRETCHING

Yoga works on exercising every muscle and counterbalancing one move with another. For instance if in one position *(asana)* you lean backwards, the next position will involve leaning forwards. Here's a simple exercise that will help you increase the flexibility of your spine and thus align your posture.

CAT AND DOG

- Kneel down and place your hands on the floor just in front of your shoulders, with your legs about hip-width apart.
- As you inhale, tilt your tailbone and pelvis up and let your spine curve down, dropping your stomach down low, pulling back your shoulders and lifting your head up. This is the dog position.
- Stretch gently.
- As you exhale, move into the cat position by reversing the spinal bend, tilting your pelvis down, moving your shoulders towards your neck, drawing your spine up and pulling in your chest and stomach.

Repeat several times, flowing smoothly from dog into cat and cat back into dog.

Chi Kung

> For me, chi kung means 'hope' because I believe it can help me become the person I want to be.
>
> **David Carradine**

The words *chi kung* mean 'skill with energy'. *Chi* is the word for energy and chi kung is all about cultivating and harnessing your own energy. It is the forerunner of the now very trendy tai chi. The advantage of chi kung over tai chi is that it's much easier to learn and it can be practised by anyone, even people who are sick or who hate the idea of exercise. If you can breathe and move your legs and/or arms gently, you can easily do chi kung.

Chi kung is based on the idea of creating a smooth flow of energy through the body. Even though you can't see energy, you can feel it. Try this exploration and see for yourself.

FEEL THE ENERGY

- Stand still with your feet apart and rub your hands vigorously together. Notice the heat you are generating. That's energy.
- Then place your right hand (if you're a man) and your left hand (if you're a woman) just a little way away from your belly, about a couple of inches below your belly button. You will notice a slightly warm feeling. That's energy too, and it has come from your body. And if you think you didn't feel something, you will. It's just a question of focus.

Think of getting dressed and trying to put your arm through a sleeve or your leg through a pair of trousers. You expect it to go through and come out the other end easily, don't you? But if that sleeve were sewn together at points along the way, you'd have a hard time reaching the other end. And you'd get a little irritated at having to break through each barrier. It is the same when you are emotionally upset for any reason – your energy collects at certain points throughout your system, clogs up the passageways, knots your muscles and bends you out of shape. It causes bad feelings, as you know, in various parts of your body.

Not many people enjoy being around people who are all knotted up, whether it's in their heads or their bodies. And if you are to have a free-flowing life with pleasant emotions running through you, your energy needs to flow freely.

Chi kung masters discovered that energy can be harnessed and directed to flow smoothly throughout the body by means of various exercises involving deep breathing, visualization, structured movement and emotional cleansing. And they're fantastic. They don't just strengthen the body and clear the mind, they are also great for getting rid of negative emotions that are stored in your muscles and joints.

All the exercises involve moving your arms and or legs away from your body and back towards it again. There's always a balance, as in yoga. You focus your mind on the centre of your body, that point below your belly button, and breathe in accordance with your movements. As you breathe in, you move your arms in one direction, and as you breathe out, they come back on themselves in some way. Doing chi kung is like rocking on a swing, pushing yourself forwards and backwards. And so you go, back and forth, in and out, very slowly and gently, feeling the energy building …

And as you do so, you use visualization. You imagine you're scooping up water and bringing it back to yourself and reaching out to touch the sky. You imagine you're a bird, lifting your arms like wings reaching out into the air and bringing them back to your body again. All the movements have lovely names like 'touching the clouds' or 'pushing mountains' or 'scooping the sea'. It makes you think of nature. I've just come back from Greece, where I did chi kung every morning standing by the ocean. That's ultimate bliss.

Here's a simple exercise for you to try it out for yourself.

A CHI KUNG TASTER

- Before you begin any chi kung exercise it's important to get comfortable and just take a moment or two to get in touch with the rhythm of your breathing and breathe deeply into your belly, as you did in the exercise above.
- Now stand with your feet about shoulder-width apart and your weight on the point just between the balls of your feet and the underside of your heels. Bend your knees ever so slightly, so they aren't locked. Let your arms hang freely by your side. Shake them out a bit.
- Gently swing your arms from side to side round the back and then round the front just to warm up.
- Stop and then slowly stretch your arms out to each side. Twist your wrists and hands backwards as you stretch your arms away from your body. Then twist your wrists the other way. This will loosen up your arms.
- Hold your arms down and a little away from your body with the fingers separated.
- Breathe into your belly and feel it expand and get soft as the air fills your lungs.

- Sense the air coming in and reaching your belly and then being dispersed all over your body and up your spine, and as you exhale, notice the energy circulating as the old air is pushed upwards out of your lungs.
- Look straight ahead and touch the roof of your mouth with your tongue.
- As you breathe in, raise your arms in front of you with the palms facing down and the hands arched as if they were tiger's claws.
- Slowly raise your arms to shoulder level. Imagine you are drawing the earth's energy upwards.
- Then, as you breathe out, bring your arms down. Feel your palms going through the air as they bring the energy back down towards your body. End with your arms just in front of your thighs.
- Do this a few times.
- Then breathe in as you raise your arms out and up to the side of your body, palms upwards, and bring your fingertips almost together at the top of your head in an arch.
- As you breathe out, bring your fingertips down, together but not touching, past the crown of your head, your forehead, your throat, your heart and your solar plexus and back to your energy centre just below the belly
- Do this a few times and then stop and think for a moment how wonderful it is to be alive and part of this big wide world.

That was just a small taster of how chi kung works. If you want to take it further, check out the Resources section (*see page 209*). The great thing is you feel good and calm and relaxed as soon as you begin. And how attractive is that?!

HARNESS THE POWER OF SOUND
Music that Moves You

Music is one of the most powerful generators of emotions and therefore of feelings in the body. My aim here is to help you to discover the music that affects different parts of your body and to use it consciously as a body-booster. It's so much easier to let positive thoughts run through your body when it has been opened out by music.

To give you an idea, when I heard *Nessun Dorma* sung by Pavarotti (most people have heard that because it was played at the 1990 Football World Cup), my heartbeat blended with the rhythm of the music and I found myself breathing deeply and slowly, as if my chest were expanding on a 360° basis. When I heard the longer drawn-out words, they seemed to pull my body in and my muscles wanted to extend even further …

Similarly, whenever I listen to *Ray of Light* by Madonna, I get a surge of feelings rising from my pelvic area into and out of my arms and I find myself wiggling my fingertips as they stretch. No wonder I like this kind of music for writing …

MUSIC TO MOVE YOU

- What music uplifts, inspires or excites you? Pick out your favourite pieces of music and listen to them with the intention of noticing how they affect your body. Feel how your body reacts as you hear the music.
- Which passages affect you the most?
- What is it about the music? You may not be able to describe it in words, but that doesn't matter.
- Notice how your body changes when you hear the music. Does it become more attractive? I suspect it does …

Music and vocals can affect us in different ways. The words of a song are first processed in the neo-cortex of our brain. That's the part that deals with language and reasoning. Then the meaning is picked up by the limbic system, which generates emotions. The vocal qualities of the words have a similar effect to the musical sound – the specific qualities of timbre, pitch, rhythm, tone and pace address a part of our brain that's much more primal. So music gets all parts of our brain working.

Tips on How to Use Music to Boost your Energy

There is plenty of music around now that's designed to create great feelings. If you like nature, then invest in sounds of the ocean or a rainforest or a summer field. They are great for relaxing and generating feelings of contentment.

There is also music that works on boosting your natural rhythm. Listen to drum music to energize and balance yourself. Better still, go to a class and try drumming. It's a great exercise in forgetting about analysing things and just following the lead of your body.

If you want to let go of incessant mind chatter, try listening to chants, African chorus singing or Tibetan bowl sounds. I listen to a piece of music by a friend of mine, Ben Scott. It consists of the sounds generated by different Tibetan bowls. The sounds hit specific energy centres of the body. As you listen to the sounds you focus on the energy centres and imagine yourself having more of each particular kind of energy. In the last chapter of this book there's a visualization and meditation exercise designed to focus on these energy centres and help you integrate your mind and body (*see page 186*).

Once you know how certain music affects your body, you can hear the music in your head and give yourself a boost anywhere!

A MUSICAL BOOST

- Find music that gives you confidence, makes you feel powerful, drives you onward or turns you on sexually. Listen to it wantonly and consciously train your body to know the feelings it generates.
- Then listen to the music in your head. Notice how the feelings come back.
- Imagine amplifying the feelings so that they get stronger, spread round your body and keep swirling in a circle, building themselves up each time.

When you do this, you will find your body generating very attractive postures!

Developing your Best Voice

Fran came to see me because she lacked confidence. She had been in a relationship for 15 years but had known right from the start that the man wasn't right for her. One of the first things I noticed about her was her voice. She had a slow measured way of talking and her voice was very weak. There was no spark in it and therefore she didn't generate a spark in me. She told me that she found it difficult in social situations. She would sit in a group and never say anything. If she started to speak she'd start to tremble and would experience what she called mild panic attacks. Often she had wanted to talk to a man but had held back. Her voice was as repressed as her feelings.

When she was at school, her English teacher had regularly singled her out to read in front of the class. If she hesitated or faltered, the teacher would make her sit down and say to the class, 'We don't want to listen to that any more, it's painful.' No wonder she found it hard to speak out.

This is not an uncommon problem. Many, many people have suppressed their natural voice because of various childhood events that have created a fear of speaking out. Things like bullying, teasing, lack of confidence-building by parents and teachers and being told to suppress emotions are all triggers for voice strangulation.

Whilst people like to know why they are the way they are, I never focus for more than a moment on that. Once people have got those 'How did this happen?' questions answered, my job is to focus on how they want to be.

When I work with people to access their Be-spot and connect with the world, amazing things happen to their voice. It becomes soft and yet very powerful. I always get a big smile on my face as I point it out to them. 'Listen to you … that sounds great.' There is a natural and powerful voice waiting inside all of us, and once again it's just a question of setting it free.

A friend of mine, Julia Williams, is a voice trainer. When people come to see her she makes a tape of their voice and then plays it back, stopping it at certain points to ask them what they notice. Surprisingly, people always seem to know what's not working with their voice. Julia also asks them to rate their voice for change of rhythm, pitch, tone and speed. And then she adds in her own experience of listening to the voice. This is a very useful exercise because it gives people an idea of the impact of their voice. You can discover the difference between a positive and negative impact with the following exploration.

POSITIVE AND NEGATIVE VOICES

Get a friend to do this with you if you can. You are going to tell them about two incidents in your life.

- Ask your friend to just listen to both stories and focus on their own body and to notice how your voice changes and how it affects them and where.
- If you can, tape record what you're saying.
- One story should be about an incident where lots of things went wrong or where you were really irritated with someone. Alternatively, think of something that you want to complain about and explain exactly what you dislike about it.
- When you've finished the 'nasty' story, get immediate feedback from your friend or play back your tape. What did you both notice?
- Pick out the bits that created the most discordant feelings and analyse what your voice was doing at the time. Did it speed up or get higher or was it venomous, as if you were spitting?
- The other story should be about a time you felt utterly uplifted, sexy, joyful, content or at peace. Choose something really positive that makes you feel very good. Tell your friend the story or record it.
- Get immediate feedback in the same way as before.
- Listen to the positive tape and mimic your voice. It's bound to sound good!

Voices often sound weak when people don't allow the full force of their emotions to seep through. The next exploration is designed to help you free up your emotions and express them vocally.

FREEING YOUR EMOTIONAL VOICE

- Here is a list of emotional states that people regularly experience: calm, happy, excited, joyful, contented, sexy, serene, lustful, playful, curious, powerful, angry, bitter, suspicious, envious, regretful. Add your own emotions to the list.
- Choose one of them and adopt a stance which expresses it. If you pick 'calm', for example, adopt a stance that feels calm. You can sit, lie down or stand up, whichever feels most appropriate.

- Then say to yourself: 'I am calm.' Say it in the calmest way you know how. If you must, pretend you are a buddha, or someone you know who is very calm. Say it in the way you'd imagine they would say it. Feel calm when you say it.
- Notice where you are getting feelings in your body. You probably want to shift your body around. Allow it to move and express itself however it wants. Follow its lead. Let it adopt a calm posture.
- Do this with all of the words in the list.

You may notice that some emotions are more difficult to express than others. Notice where you hold back. If you're not much cop *yet* at expressing positive emotions, great! Now you know what you need to focus on. If you find it more difficult to express negative emotions, ask yourself whether you are suppressing these emotions. Of course it might just be that you don't have room for those emotions in your life and rarely get angry, envious or resentful, etc. *Great!* You're a shining example to others.

Everyone has the potential to develop a great voice and to speak out freely and with passion. You can learn a lot here from other people. While you watch TV or listen to the radio, pay attention to the way people speak. Listen out for the changes in tone and rhythm. Notice where they put the inflections and which words they draw out or shorten. Be aware of when they speak quickly and when they slow down. Listen to the way their voice changes in relation to the subject matter. And then mimic, mimic, mimic.

The more you immerse yourself in great voice, the greater your chances of being able to give great voice. And that's a juicy thought.

ENERGETIC FLEXIBILITY

Have you noticed how you get irritated or uncomfortable in the presence of some people even before they've started talking? And how with others everything just feels right?

The energy we give out affects everyone around us and the effect can be either positive or negative. For example, I used to be so enthusiastic about things that I'd rush right up to people and just bombard them. Some people loved it and responded with equal gusto, but others seemed to withdraw from it. Those who withdrew were all quiet by nature. My energy was too much of a contrast to theirs. When I realized this it opened out a whole new world for me. I began to notice how different people were.

If you want to have a positive effect on the people you approach, you have to learn what I call 'energetic flexibility'. But first it might be useful to know what kind of energy you give out.

WHAT KIND OF ENERGY ARE YOU?

Look at the following descriptions and decide which matches you best. For every positive quality, there is also a contrasting overload quality. You can also have fun matching the types to the people you know well.

Earth

Rich and Earthy Garden: Fertile, nurturing, growing at a measured pace. My partner is very earthed. He is great to be around and calms down my rather wild energy without holding it back. He gives me room to grow.

Frosty. Stony Ground: Rigid, inflexible, stubborn, holding back. When you're around someone like this, it's impossible to crack them. They don't bend to meet other people and stick to their own ways. You don't feel as if you can flourish in their presence.

Water

Riding the Waves: Flowing, free, smooth, powerful. Runners, pole-vaulters, acrobats, ice skaters, dancers and some footballers have this kind of energy. So does my friend Lesley, who seems to glide into every situation and take it all in her stride. Her elegance is very attractive.

A Swirling Typhoon: Destructive, overwhelming, overpowering. Do you know someone who storms around, overwhelms everyone and rides roughshod over them to get their own way?

Fire

Log Fire on a Winter's Day: Warm, energized, comforting. There are some people you warm to easily. When you are around them their warmth envelops you, their enthusiasm fires you up and you feel gently energized. My mother's doctor is like that. She says she always feels uplifted when she meets her.

Forest Fire out of Control: All-consuming, burning, destructive. Perhaps you've met people who seem to rush around, do everything far too quickly and leave a trail of destruction in their wake, often not realizing what they've done.

Air

Gentle or Energizing Breeze: Floating, soft, light, gentle, energizing, reviving. These people seem to float in and out of your life leaving you feeling energized yet with a sense of calm and lightness. They give out an uplifting and playful vibe.

Whirlwind: Swirling, wild, sweeping past you. Perhaps you've met people like that too – you'll know if you have! They rush in and disturb everyone without a thought for the mess they scatter around them.

What are you most like? Most of us are a mixture of the two qualities of our particular element. What about your friends and the people around you? Notice how they move and affect other people. Have fun with it!

Games to Enhance your Energetic Flexibility

One of the things that people find very attractive in others is when they show they've listened and understood what they are saying. Energetic flexibility is the key to this. When you can talk someone's language with both words and body, you will appear more attractive to them. Imagine how useful this would be. And you would be able to communicate so much more clearly as well! The following games are designed to enhance your energetic flexibility with both words and body language.

TEN-MINUTE DISCOVERY GAME

Get a friend to do this with you. Ask them if they've got 10 minutes to help you pay more attention to people when they're talking to you. Explain to them that all they have to do is tell you a few times about a super-duper memorable moment in their lives. Pick someone you know will be up for it! They'll immediately think about super-duper moments in their life, feel good and be flattered that you're interested in them.

- Find somewhere quiet and comfortable.
- Ask your friend if they are comfortable. (It's important to make people feel comfortable.)
- Position yourself opposite them. Make sure you're comfortable too.
- Ask your friend to tell you about a super-duper memorable moment in their life.
- Don't try to memorize it all, just enjoy the experience.
- As they tell you the story, notice the following *and* adopt them yourself:

Posture: How are they positioned? Notice the position of their spine, shoulders, legs, arms, hands, feet, neck and head. Check their symmetry and asymmetry. Look for any leaning gestures or clenching of hands or feet.

Gestures: Notice how they move their hands, legs, head, shoulders, etc.

Rhythm: Do they tap or shake their head in some kind of rhythm?

Location of gestures: Where do they put their hands?

Facial gestures: Notice any movements involving tongue, lips, eyes, nostrils, forehead and eyebrows.

Gesture and word links: Where do their gestures occur in relation to what they're saying? Try to get the words or phrases that link to each particular gesture. Notice how the gestures begin and when they end.

Breathing changes: Look at where their body rises and falls when they breathe and harmonize your breathing in time with theirs. This isn't an intellectual exercise. Feel the changes.

- *Listen.* If you notice yourself focusing on a lack of detail or thinking there's too much information, make a mental note of it and then get back to listening. There's always time to ask questions later and focusing on them now will deflect your attention from the story.
- If you have to ask questions, do so only to clarify: 'Can you tell me what you mean by ...? Could you just tell me that again? How does that connect?'
- When they have finished, thank them.
- Make eye contact.
- Take in a deep breath to your belly and let it out slowly. As you breathe in, pay attention to your belly and then let it out.
- Imagine that for a moment you are your friend. Play their story back in your head. Listen to their words, see their gestures, feel their energy.
- Then retell their story to them. Use their tone of voice and their gestures where you can. If they told their story quickly and with energy, you tell it like that too. If they told it slowly, in a laid-back fashion, get laid back yourself.
- Watch them as you speak.

  Notice when they react to what you say.
  Notice when you think they are giving signs of disagreement.
  Notice when they are giving signs but you're not sure what they mean.

- Be prepared to stop and ask, 'Is that right? Is that how it is?'
- If necessary, let them tell you again. (Relax, people love reliving memorable moments!)
- Go on for as long as it's fun.

EMOTIONAL CHARADES

As you now know, people express their emotions in a very specific way in their bodies. In this game you are going to act out the way other people 'do' emotions. This will develop your emotional flexibility and enhance your ability to empathize. It may also help you to understand that everyone is different and encourage you to be more open-minded.

- Get a group of people together, or just one friend if you prefer.
- Make a list of emotions you want to act out (preferably positive emotions).
- Write each item on a different piece of paper and put them all in a pile.
- Take it in turns to select and act out an emotion. Do not use words or sounds. Use only your body.
- As one person acts out the emotion, another person stands opposite them and copies them. (The rest of the group can enjoy watching you both.)
- The person copying has to guess what the emotion is.
- When they have guessed correctly, they can ask the other person, 'What does [the emotion] mean to you?'
- Listen to their reply and pay attention to how they say it. This will be useful when you are working on verbal communication in the next chapter.

AWAKENING YOUR SEXUALITY
How Is It for You?

In order to be truly attractive our energy needs to flow smoothly, and this includes sexual energy. Remember how when we do yoga breathing or chi kung we keep our focus on that spot just below the navel? Sexual and creative energy generates here and sends itself round the body. When we hold back our emotions and contract our bodies, we make it difficult for that energy to flow.

How is it for you right now? Does your sexuality express itself like a limp lettuce leaf or a weak cup of tea? Or do you see sex as a kind of orgasm Olympics, as you strive for more variety, novelty and orgasms? If you are holding yourself back *or* trying too hard, chances are you won't be experiencing sexual bliss. We all have enormous potential for sexual bliss, which we can enjoy on our own or with someone else. We just have to let go of the stuff that's held us back for so long.

Tanya told me that as a young girl she was very attractive. She always had men coming on to her and felt uncomfortable about it. Eventually she was so overwhelmed by the onslaught of attention that she closed off and created a protective shell. She began to hold back her natural expression and monitor the things she said and did.

The few times she did get involved in a sexual relationship, she found herself holding back. She was scared of her own power. Then on the day before her fortieth birthday, she suddenly felt very sad. She realized that as a result of her actions she had deprived herself of a truly intimate relationship with a man. She had plenty of men friends, but friendship was where it stopped.

Tanya had to learn to get in touch with her sexuality again and realize that it's healthy to be sexually attractive. She also had to accept that you don't have to flaunt your sexuality in order to be sexual.

■ ■ ■

George had a series of relationships with women but most of them didn't last longer than a year or two. George was an accountant, a logical kind of guy and a keen sportsman. He liked to keep himself fit and he wanted to be a sexual athlete too, but he wondered why his sexual experiences were never the earth-shattering event that he'd read about in the glossy mags.

George spent too much time in his head working out the right thing to do to 'give' his partner an orgasm. When I first met him I noticed that he was very measured and controlled in both his verbal and body language. He might have been a technically good lover but he had disconnected from his emotions. Passion is a very powerful emotion and when we sever the connection between our passion and our sexuality we miss out on ecstasy.

■ ■ ■

Kit told me about her lover, who was very similar to George. When he ditched her for a younger model, she had a fling with Carlo, who was 15 years younger. She said that although Carlo wasn't as skilled as her former lover, he was fired up with passion. She said his passion really turned her on and she felt as if she had permission to unleash her wild side. She described sex with Carlo as all-encompassing and her orgasms as much more powerful.

When we first make love to someone, we're often at the lust stage, fired up by an excess of raging hormones. We don't need much to get us going. It's our

DNA, ensuring survival. If sexual desire declines as a relationship grows, it's often because we've relied on that lust-fuelled passion to keep us going. Have you ever wondered why people enjoy sex so much after a good row? It's because arguing generates all kinds of emotional activity in the body, including passion. It's a way of bringing the body alive. And it's a bit of a roundabout painful way if you ask me. Wouldn't it be much more powerful to be able to generate passion *without* having to argue?

When you reconnect to the richness of your own passion, you will notice how the quality of your sexual experience changes. One of the most powerful ways to reawaken this connection is tantra.

Tantra

Tantra is an ancient spiritual path that is older than most religions. It doesn't require you to believe in anything, it simply asks you to be willing to explore your inner world. It is an outlook, a method and a way of life that helps people to open their hearts, embrace their sexuality and celebrate the whole of life whilst recognizing that everyone has a touch of the divine. It is about a lot more than multiple orgasms and delayed ejaculation, although sexual bliss *is* easily reached when you practise it. Tantra is about finding spirituality through sexuality and having a whale of a good time into the bargain! And there is something very sensual and alluring about people who have taken the tantra path. They seem to exude sexuality and ease at the same time.

I decided to explore tantra with Leora Lightwoman. She teaches a Buddhist-derived form of tantra which she calls Diamond Light Tantra. The classes are a mixture of couples and single people but always gender balanced. I was surprised at first to see so many single people, but that was before I realized what tantra was really about. I had a lot of powerful experiences during the weekend and got a stronger sense of how sexual energy can be used to enhance creativity, love and bliss.

Tantra is very strong on love that delves beneath the surface of physical looks. It connects with those 'divine' qualities we all have. It's really empowering to look into the eyes of another person and think of them as a god or goddess, a Shiva or Shakti. You can't help but feel good towards them.

When we accept ourselves as beautiful just the way we are and enter deeply into every aspect of our lives, including our sexuality, our hearts and minds expand and unite to create physical and emotional bliss. Everyone can achieve this bliss! And whether you want to dip your toes into tantra or dive into it as a way of life, you can experience the power that comes from releasing your sexual energy. If you feel drawn to this path, I suggest you seek out the guidance of a qualified teacher. Meanwhile, I invite you to come with me to the water's edge and dip your toes into the river of your own sexuality.

FREEING UP YOUR SEXUAL ENERGY

How comfortable are you with your own naked body? Do you avoid looking in a full-length mirror or do you delight in admiring the wonder of your body? Check it out for yourself – it's a great eye-opener.

- Stand naked in front of a full-length mirror and check how you feel.
- Are you carrying around a load of issues about sexuality which fetter you and hold you back?
- Do you feel alive, open and free or are there feelings of guilt, shame and shyness?

Whatever you feel about your body, and ultimately your sexuality, is what your lover will experience when they make love to you.

Not so pleasant sexual experiences, shame about sex and fears all cause the body to be tense. It's perfectly possible to have a sexual experience even when we are tense and therefore contracted, but the experience is more likely to be confined to the genital area. When we relax and expand our body, we allow the energy to travel. When our sexual energy has free passage it can spread those exquisite sexual feelings to our entire body.

The following exercise helps to shake out tensions throughout the body and generates a powerful energy pulse. As you do it, just notice what comes up for you. Whatever it is, it's OK. All feelings are valid. There is no right or wrong … just the doing. You may notice some pleasurable feelings. Certainly I've found the more I do this exercise, the more it generates very pleasant sensations. Everyone experiences it in their own way.

LEORA'S KUNDALINI SHAKING

- Close your eyes and breathe into your belly, filling it with energy, and then relax as you exhale.
- With your feet planted firmly on the ground, relax your jaw and your mouth.
- Imagine there's some movement beneath you, causing your knees to shake. Let them shake up and down, backwards and forwards. Feel the vibration in your knees.
- Continue to do this for a while.
- Then, still with your feet firmly planted on the floor, let the vibrations rise up to your hips.
- Notice how your hips begin to shake and your pelvis moves backwards and forwards and from side to side.
- Shake out any tension in your legs and hips.
- Continue to do this for a while.
- Then let the vibrations extend to your back. Let your back undulate and move in different directions as it shakes along with your hips and knees. Notice how the movement in your back frees up tensions there.
- Relax your jaw, your shoulders and your belly.
- Let the shaking rise up into your shoulders and shake out any tension you hold there.
- Now just let go and allow your whole body to shake.
- Notice any areas that feel good and breathe into them.
- Notice any sounds that want to come out. Sighs, groans shouts – whatever comes up is right for you. Let it out.
- Let your whole body shake for as long as feels good. Feel that sense of aliveness.
- Then slowly allow the shaking to calm down, starting on the inside.
- Notice your energy flowing on the inside.
- As you come to a stop, notice how energized you feel.

Practise this regularly and you will really loosen up and prepare yourself to generate powerful sexual energy that will enhance your creativity and sense of power.

MEN AND WOMEN

Men tend to think with their genitals whilst women think with their hearts. One of the aims of tantra is to link sexuality to love so that men and women can experience the joy of love flowing into sexuality together with sexuality expressing itself through the heart.

To do this, men have to learn to connect to their emotions and feel from their heart and women have to learn to channel their feelings of love through sexuality. Try it – it's a great way to help you connect.

CONNECTING LOVE AND SEX

- Stand in front of the mirror and place one hand on your heart and one hand between your legs, clasping your genitals.
- If you are a man, think sexy thoughts until you start to get that familiar stirring in your loins.
- Notice the sensations around your genital area and imagine them moving up your back and into your heart.
- Focus on your heart and think about times when you've felt real love. It doesn't have to be romantic love. Notice the feelings in your heart area ...
- Then imagine this energy moving back down through your stomach into your genitals.
- If you are a woman, start by focusing on your heart.
- Generate all those easily aroused feelings of deep love and affection. Notice the sensations around your heart area.
- Then imagine this energy going down through your belly into your genitals. Loop it back up again through your back into your heart.

The more you practise this looping and joining of love to sexuality, the more complete you'll feel.

When you feel good about yourself, you'll find it much easier to share your desires, fantasies and needs with your partner.

If you want to explore the art of charismatic communication, turn the page and let's get chattin' ...

CHAPTER 6

CHARISMATIC COMMUNICATION

Words are, of course, the most powerful drug used by
mankind.

Rudyard Kipling

Mr Kipling was spot on. Over the years people have used carefully crafted
language to lead nations to war, initiate peace movements, change laws, sell
products and generally inspire, motivate, entertain and amuse. Charismatic
communication can turn everyday words into magic wands – and influence and
interest people and draw them to you. You'd be crazy not to want that, wouldn't
you?

But first let's see how you rate right now in the charismatic communication
stakes. Are you a firm favourite or are you a rank outsider? You know the truth.

HOW DO YOU COMMUNICATE?

How do you rate yourself as a communicator? Are you effective, powerful
and attractive, or is there room for improvement? The questions below
are intended to make you think about how you communicate, what you
communicate, how well you appear to be understood *and* where some
improvement is required! As you read them through, pay attention to
those scenarios that seem to leap out from the page. Notice how your
body reacts and what thoughts you generate.

- First of all, take a quick trip down memory lane to your schooldays.

  Were you ever asked to read out loud or perform to the class? Was it torture or did you enjoy it or was it somewhere in between?
  Did the teacher ever praise you or tell you off in front of the class?
  Just notice whether this brings back unpleasant or pleasant feelings and then let them go and come back to the present.

- Have you ever had a conversation where you felt that you were really in tune with the other person and they were in tune with you?

  What were they doing?
  What were you doing?

- Have you ever had times when you felt as if you were having a big communication clash with someone?

  What is it that they said or did that didn't work for you?
  What might you have been doing differently from them?

- Are people rapt when you are talking or do you notice their attention wandering?
- Do you find yourself regularly being asked to explain what you mean?
- Do people respond to you in a way that leads you to believe they haven't got a clue what you're talking about? And more to the point, are you noticing this?
- Do you sometimes find it difficult to speak up?
- When you think about public speaking, do you:

  Get that sinking feeling and start to shake. It's your greatest fear.
  Feel nervous because you're not as good as you'd like to be in front of a group.
  Get excited because you *love* it.

- What would it be like to stand up in front of a group and talk in such a way that you hold their attention and make them laugh and afterwards people come up to you and say, 'That was great'?

- When you are in a group, do you find yourself leading conversations or are you waiting for someone else to lead you?
- When you talk to other people, do you sometimes think to yourself, 'That's not what I meant to say'?
- When someone else is talking, are you hearing *all* of what they're saying or are you analysing, making judgements or planning what you want to say in return?
- How does it affect you when you make a statement and someone gives back a distorted analysis of it? Are you sometimes guilty of this yourself?
- Has anyone ever said to you, *'Listen* to me!' or 'You're not listening!'?
- Do you tailor your conversation to suit the person you're talking to or do you think, 'Take me as you find me'?
- Do you find it easy to persuade people to do things? How would you like more of that on tap?
- Are there words or phrases that you use to excess?
- Are you a fast talker or do you tend to speak ... more ... sloooowly?
- Do you find it easier to converse with someone who puts in lots of detail or someone who paints a big picture?
- When you start a conversation with someone new, do you put aside thoughts of how you might impress them and instead concentrate on finding out about them?

Now say 'Yippee!' because whatever 'failings' you think you have discovered, there are going to be potent opportunities for you to develop into a charismatic communicator. And as a charismatic communicator you'll find it easy to:

develop and maintain a positive attitude towards yourself and others
know what you want and expect the best
make others feel comfortable, safe and relaxed with you
get others to open out to you
pay close attention
gather information
use the information to communicate in a way that's personally compelling to
    people

I'm going to give you some great insights and tips to get you started.

CHARISMATIC COMMUNICATION 101: BASIC SKILLS

Pretend that every single person you meet has a sign around his or her neck that says: 'Make Me Feel Important.' Not only will you succeed in sales, you will succeed in life.

Mary Kay Ash

What are charismatic communicators like? They are attractive. They make it easy for people to interact with them. They know how to make someone feel important, comfortable and most of all *heard*.

Attractive communicators judge the accuracy of what they've said by the response they get. If what comes back isn't what they expected, they realize they've been misunderstood and they make it their responsibility to change what they say and how they say it until they get their meaning across.

Attractive communicators always seek clarification if they don't quite understand something. They are always alert to how easy it is to just assume. They are always prepared to use the golden nugget question: 'What do you mean by …?'

Attractive communicators know that whilst well-structured language can be mind-blowingly powerful, it's useless without the right attitude and approach. They have a caring and positive attitude towards the people they're talking to, no matter what the content of the communication. They always want the person to enjoy the communication and they want it to be mutually beneficial. They expect the best.

Common Sense

Most of charismatic communication seems like basic common sense. It is. But sadly, we don't always apply common sense. That's when we need a swift reminder.

One girl in my class told me that what I was teaching was common sense. I agreed with her. I told her about Paul, a client who had a really hard time making eye contact. What was common sense to some people was not at all obvious to Paul. But when eventually he found the courage to look up and meet someone's eyes, it changed his whole world for the better.

So remember, as you read on, that sometimes the simplest little thing can make a huge difference.

Be Curious about People

Do you think of contact with people as a dangerous journey with perils around each corner? Or do you think of each encounter as an adventure of discovery? Great communicators see other people as potential playmates or teachers or connections. They tell themselves that whatever happens it's going to be worthwhile, because they're going to learn something valuable. This gives them the courage to initiate new contacts and sets them up for success.

They are also curious about people. They want to know what makes them tick. But when they feel themselves starting to make judgements, they take that as a signal to let go and search for more information. They tend to give second and third chances because they know it takes time and effort to get a good feel for someone and paint a true picture. And that everyone is interesting when you press the right buttons …

Know What You Want and Expect the Best

All great communicators understand the power of focused expectation. When you keep in mind what kind of response you're after, you will find it much easier to lead the conversation in that direction. But you have to really believe you're going to get what you want.

Angie came to see me because she wanted to get married after five years of living with her partner, but when I asked her, 'What do you expect to happen?' her answer was quite different. She said, 'He might worry about losing his freedom and get scared off.' Angie's expectations did not match her desires and that can cause problems, because your expectations will determine what you get.

When I asked Angie, 'What has to happen to make marriage to Tom more likely?', she came up with two ideas: 'Maybe I could stop asking him where he's been every time he goes out and trust him a bit more' and 'Maybe I should let him have more time to himself and learn to do some things on my own.'

I asked her, 'How will that make it more likely to get what you want?' Her reply said it all: 'If Tom feels free when he's with me, he's going to be more open to marriage because he won't be so scared of losing his freedom.'

Obviously, when someone else is involved, there's never a guarantee that they will go along with what you want. But when you learn to think like this, you're seriously increasing your chances of success.

There's an old saying: 'Energy follows thought.' This suggests, quite rightly in my experience, that whatever you focus on finding is what you will find. So before you open your mouth, you may find it useful to build up an optimistic focus.

BUILDING AN OPTIMISTIC FOCUS

- If there is something important that you wish to say to someone you are close to, I suggest you start by reminding yourself that there are some very good reasons why you are close to this person.
- Take a moment or two to think loving thoughts of them, even if you are experiencing some anger or other unpleasant emotion towards them right now.
- Let go of the old thoughts and just look around you. Pay attention to what's happening, check out how your body feels and relax.
- Then look at or think about the person you are about to communicate with. Send them some more loving thoughts.
- If this is a communication with someone you have to reprimand in some way, maybe in a business or social context, remind yourself that this person is doing the best they can given all that has gone to make them the way they are today. You may not know their history so you won't be able to imagine why they are doing what they are doing. Instead, just imagine that they have potential and that they do want to succeed.
- Let go of any judgements and blame and think of how you want them to be. Keep this in mind so that you can use your linguistic wizardry to lead them away from murky thoughts towards somewhere much more open and ripe for constructive action.
- If this is a business negotiation, remind yourself of what you already know. The best outcome in any negotiation is always win-win. Keep this firmly in mind.

- How much do you know about the other person's hopes and expectations? Keep asking yourself 'What's in it for them?' and 'What has to happen to make it work'? This focuses your mind away from barriers towards solutions and valuable results.
- If your mind keeps bringing up those imaginary barriers, ask yourself: 'What has to happen to dissolve, drive through or sail round the barriers?'
- Take an imaginary step into their shoes. See yourself through their eyes and hear yourself communicating to them. What do you think is most important to them? Are you making it attractive to them?

This should help build up an optimistic attitude. We'll work on the linguistic skills later.

The Comfort Factor

Attractive communicators know that when people feel comfortable, they're much more open to suggestion. Here are a few hints on how to make people feel relaxed.

MAKE THEM FEEL AT HOME

Pick the right place to talk. You might be happy to discuss personal stuff in the coffee room, but not everyone is. If you are about to communicate sensitive information, reprimand someone or ask them personal questions, pick a place where you can't be overheard.

When someone else enters your space, it gives you the upper hand. Don't abuse it. As the host, it's your place to make it easy for a guest to feel 'at home' in your environment. Don't flaunt your power and sit behind your desk, for example, unless you deliberately want them to feel uncomfortable.

Similarly, if you are on their home ground, make up your mind to feel at home no matter what they do. Take responsibility for your own feelings and sense of personal power. Say to yourself, 'If it is to be, it is up to me.'

GET ON THE RIGHT SIDE OF THEM

I mean this literally. Most of us have a side on which it feels more comfortable to have other people stand or sit. Sometimes we aren't even aware of it, we just sense a little more discomfort if they're on the wrong side.

So, if possible, let a person sit or stand or loll where they feel most comfortable. Wait till they're settled and then ask them whether they'd be more comfortable with you on their right or left. A simple 'Would you prefer it if I sat here or there?' as you indicate each spot will do it.

If you are someone who tries to please other people too much, however, or always lets other people choose, you might want to take this opportunity to go for what makes *you* comfortable.

EQUALIZE WITH THEM

People who have an affinity with kids can often be found on the floor at 'kid level'. They're more into having fun with the kid than maintaining their status as superior adults. If you want to create equality in your communication, sit or stand beside someone on the same level. After all, you're OK about who you are, aren't you? You don't need to put someone down or hide behind a fancy desk, do you?

WATCH THEIR SPACE

Before you approach someone, smile and make eye contact first. This tells them you're friendly and safe. Don't rush in and stand too close or 'in their face', or sneak up on them or take them by surprise, as you will step over the boundaries of their personal space. This is the distance we all need to keep between ourselves and another person. The amount we require varies. If we like a person and know them well, we will let them get much closer than a stranger can.

Be aware of a person's personal space. If you dive in too close too quickly, they will feel invaded. Constantly check for 'space invasion imminent' warning signs. These are the signals that occur just *before* a person contracts and moves back. Small facial muscle changes, narrowing eyes and moving the chin backwards are all signs flashing up the message 'Get any closer and I'm moving back.' (See more detailed information on signals later on in this chapter.)

One good way to experiment with moving closer to people is to move gently in and out of their space. Make sure you are smiling and make brief but regular eye contact, then take a small step towards them and move backwards again. Continue to do this from time to time, moving a little bit closer each time. The small steps acclimatize a person to you and make them more willing to let you into their space.

People do all sorts of things in their personal space, including using the area in front of them like a projection screen. When they're thinking about the future and possibilities, they tend to glance in front. So if you sit or stand directly in front of them, you could be in the space they use for viewing the contents of their mind's eye! When you want someone to access their bliss spot or get a good picture of something you're proposing, stand or sit beside them to allow them a clear line of sight ahead.

Read their Signals

You can't be a great communicator without being a great people reader. Attractive communicators are super-detectives of human signals. They're alert to every little shift. So, how open are you to what's going on? Many of us have developed a kind of protective bubble that keeps the world out. If you live in a busy city you will know the unnerving feeling of scurrying down a quiet street at dusk or being stuck in the middle of a crowd of drunks on a Saturday night. It's not surprising we shut down. There are times when we don't want to notice things and we don't want to be noticed.

This is a protective mechanism and it works well when you use it selectively. What sometimes happens, though, is that we filter out the world. And it is not a good way to be if you need to pick up signals. Tune back in with the following exercise.

SHARPEN UP YOUR SENSES

■ Take five days and every day make up your mind to use one sense more consciously.

Day 1: Look out for things. Notice what you see.
Day 2: Listen for sounds going on around you.
Day 3: Pay attention to bodily sensations.
Day 4: Sniff things out – what smells do you notice?
Day 5: Get a taste for life. What tastes do you come into contact with? What tastes do you get in your mouth?

■ Also, practise the body-awareness exercises (see page 44), notice when you're not paying attention and spend more time being present.

People often ask me what signals they should look out for and I say with a smile, 'Anything that changes!' Here are some useful types of change to look out for and some very general ideas as to what they *could* mean. Remember, though, to be open to more than the obvious interpretation. There's a great advert on British TV which shows a guy wearing pretty scruffy clothing and looking quite dishevelled running crazily towards someone. He has a determined look on his face. You immediately imagine he's going to attack the person. And then the camera angle switches and you see him pushing them out of the way of falling scaffolding. Things aren't always as they seem.

FORWARDS MOVEMENT

This could be a sign that a person is paying more attention or that they are on the alert for action. It could also mean that they can't hear well or even that they are trying to get a closer whiff of your perfume!

BACKWARDS MOVEMENT

Sometimes people move back when they want to think about something. It's as if they need to give themselves more distance. This may be because it's too much to contemplate all at once or because they sense a threat (real or imagined).

CROSSING LIMBS

Sometimes people cross their limbs when they've received information that makes them uncomfortable or warns them they need more time to think. It may be a stalling tactic. When you cross your limbs, you are making it more difficult for the energy to flow. If you are trying to figure out a problem or to come unstuck from something, crossing your limbs could hinder you.

RHYTHMICAL MOVEMENT

Notice any rhythmical movements people make when they're talking. If they have a jagged rhythm or are very frenetic, that's generally a hint that they're having some thoughts that aren't that useful. If their rhythm is paced and even, such as a gentle but slight nodding of the head or moving up and down of a foot, this generally indicates they're enjoying something pleasant. When people talk about how they are at their best, they often fall into a rhythm as they experience it.

HAND MOVEMENT

Pay particular attention to the hands. They are one of the most expressive parts of our body, as anyone who has seen Italians talk will agree!

As we feel the urge to speak our hands often move. Sometimes when someone is about to speak but loses the opportunity you will see a hand somewhere up around their face. Look out for hands being moved upwards or outwards. Sometimes people make a little gesture like this and then pull their hands back. This might be a sign that they want to say something. Or they might be thinking something and then have stopped themselves for some reason.

People also use their hands to mark out things in the space around them. They'll put their hands in a particular location when they're describing something. A common example of this is when someone talks about 'putting something behind them' and moves their hands in a backwards movement.

A skilled communicator will be asking questions that get people into all sorts of states and will watch as they mark them all out in the space around them. For example, when Sandy talked about a 'fantastic opportunity', he lifted his left hand with the palm up and curled his fingers inwards, then moved his arm back and then forwards and stopped with a jolt. He was mapping out his representation of 'fantastic opportunity'. And being aware of what he did would be useful in getting him to think about future fantastic opportunities.

THE FACE

The face is a very telling organ and it talks incessantly. We are all familiar with obvious facial movements like raised eyebrows and a downturned mouth. But what about the not so obvious ones?

Skin-colour Change

Skin colour can change with emotion. When someone is 'hot around the collar' they're experiencing a temperature rise and increased blood flow in the neck. These changes are common in the cheeks, the neck and the area just below. Conversely, people can go 'as white as a sheet', when there is a noticeable drain of blood from the surface of the skin. Provided there isn't a sudden rush of icy wind or a rapid rise in temperature, or the person isn't about to keel over because they're physically ill, you can assume that the skin colour change is due to a powerful emotion.

Minute Muscle Movement

People make many unconscious micro-muscular movements. When you can detect these, you're getting early-warning information about change.

Pay particular attention to the nose and the mouth. People tend move their mouth and nose from side to side very slightly when they're sizing up something or trying to make a decision. They may also incline their head in opposite directions.

The muscles of the mouth move a lot even when we're not saying anything. Generally upwards movements are more likely to indicate a positive thought than downwards movements.

Notice how the forehead muscles twitch before someone frowns or raises their eyebrows.

I've noticed quite a lot of my clients licking their lips as they're accessing their Bliss-spot. Often their tongue pokes out just a tiny bit and then retreats. When I point it out to them, they are often quite unaware of having done it. Sometimes I just say, 'Is that tasty?' ... and they light up.

Multi-tasking Eyes

I'm not at all surprised that the eyes are referred to as the windows to the soul. Not only do they express the widest range of emotions, from absolute contempt to deep love, but they also move around in very specific ways as we take in and process information from the outside world.

As you ask someone a question, pay particular attention to where their gaze goes. People cast their gaze in different directions depending on what emotions and thoughts they are accessing and what they're feeling in their body. As you've discovered when accessing your Be-spot, when you look in a certain direction, it sets off a chain reaction in your body.

People also use their eyes to visualize things in the space around them. It's like one big cinema out there. When people create images in their mind's eye, it's as if they're projecting it somewhere in the space around them. You can sometimes see someone look out and then move their eyes (and body) back. They're moving back from the image they see or trying to step out of it to get more distance – just like me nowadays when I read!

People also move their eyes to specific locations when they're doing specific things such as remembering or talking to themselves. When you hear a noise, unbeknown to you, your eyes will move in the direction of it. The same thing happens when you talk to yourself – your eyes move towards your ears. They might move to the left or right or go back and forth between the two. If you notice someone doing this it means they're having an internal dialogue. When I notice clients doing this I might say to them, 'So what *are* you saying to yourself?' They look surprised, as if I've read their minds, but I'm not telepathic, just very observant!

Often when people want to visualize, they look up and to their left and right. Don't mistake this as a lack of attention because they've not looking at *you*. They simply need to look up to enhance their ability to visualize. They'll look down when they're ready. Be patient. If it's appropriate you can ask, 'So what does that look like to you?' or 'How does that seem?'

When we look down we are often thinking. I was teaching a class a while back and noticed one of the participants looked down most of the time. When I asked her if she'd had trouble at school, she nodded. 'The teachers always accused me of not paying attention and told me to look up.' But it was obvious that looking down helped her think. It was her way of learning. In the same way, when someone looks down, give them time, they're just thinking.

And when most people are accessing un-useful thoughts, they'll gaze in a specific direction. Knowing this can be very useful. When people begin to display signs of emotions bubbling up, notice where they are looking. Sometimes by redirecting their line of sight you can avoid them becoming overwhelmed by unpleasant emotions.

PRE-SIGNALS

Some of the above are 'pre-signals' to the more obvious body language we're used to noticing. They're useful because sometimes by the time you get the obvious signals, it's too late. The opportunity is missed, or worse still, the damage is done.

Take personal space invasion. When I ask people, 'How do you know you're too close?', they always say, 'The other person moves back.' And I reply, 'And then it's too late, you've invaded their space. If you are able to pick up the signals they give out *before* they move back, you'll be able to stop yourself invading.' When moving closer to people, be on the alert for slight changes in the eyes, often an almost imperceptible narrowing. Watch out for the chin moving back towards the neck. When you get those signals, *stop*.

Picking up the early formative signals always puts you ahead of the game. You get more time to take immediate action, change what you're doing or accommodate yourself to what's to come. That split-second can make or break a communication.

The Opening Moves

Communication is like a game of chess – you have to be aware of the potential moves and the effect they can have not just on the moment, but on the entire game. Each move you make will influence the move the other person makes and vice versa. If you make the first move, you are showing them the way and opening the channels.

The opening moves of any communication are vital. Get them right and you'll go far ...

You know what it's like when you are on your way out of the door and the phone rings – you pick up the phone or give them your attention because it might be something important and before you can say 'I'm on my way out' or 'I haven't any time right now' they launch into a long tirade. Meanwhile you're tapping your toes or looking at your watch and thinking about where you've got to be and how you might be late. The last thing on your mind is what they're saying to you. If only they'd taken the time to ask if you had the time.

You can create a feel-good situation for people who find it difficult to stop and say 'Not a good time right now.' A simple courtesy question can make or break a communication. Before you begin to talk, check that it's convenient with these questions:

'Is this a good time for you?'
'Can you spare me a few minutes to talk about ...?' (and make sure if you say ten minutes you don't ramble on for half an hour!)
'Can you talk?'
'There's something I want to discuss with you and it's important, is now a good time?'

If you do this, the other person will feel respected. They'll feel warm and open towards you. And even if they don't have time, they'll feel OK about saying so and will be more likely to agree to talk to you another time.

If they don't have time to talk right now, make sure you find out when they will:

'When would be a good time?'
'Would you be able to talk tomorrow/next week?'
'Can I call you this afternoon?'
'Would it help if I called your secretary and made an appointment with her?'

Get some commitment to further action, no matter how small, and then let them go on their way.

BEFOREPLAY QUESTIONS

Of course 'Is this a good time to talk?' won't be the only question you might want to ask. And sometimes just asking a question directly can be a little harsh. That's why good communicators use what I call 'question foreplay'.

These phrases are a gentle way of leading into a question:

'I'm curious to know whether ...'
'Would you share with me ...?'
'I'd appreciate your telling me ...'
'I wonder whether ...'
'I hope you won't mind telling me ...'

The following phrases give the impression that you're asking permission to ask a question:

'I wonder if you'd mind me asking ...?'
'Can I ask you a question ...?'
'Would it be OK for me to ask you ...?
'I'd like to ask you a bit more about ...'
'There's something I want to clarify, so would you be able to answer a couple of questions?'
'Would you mind if I asked you ...?'

All of these will help put people at their ease. As will a little chit-chat.

THE POWER OF CHIT-CHAT

When I was training to be a facilitator and therapist, I was taught the importance of starting every encounter with a casual conversation. Chit-chat, as I call it, puts people at their ease. It is a great form of social lubrication. It reduces tension and helps people relax and open out, and if you're paying attention and ask the right questions, it can give you a real insight into their patterns of motivation. Chit-chat can be a really powerful communication tool.

I am particularly fond of 'agreeable chit-chat', or the art of getting someone to nod their head. Sales people call it the 'yes set'. When you get someone to agree with you about simple things, they're much more likely to agree with the important stuff.

Keep your ears and eyes open for an opening. You can talk about your journey, the weather, the place you are in, new laws, traffic, living in town/the country/by the sea, seasonal events or any frivolous current event. Here are a few ideas:

- *If someone has a dog or a child:* 'Oh, isn't he/she lovely? What a gorgeous baby/dog/child!'
- *If there's something particularly outstanding, like the child's great hair or the dog's lovely markings:* 'Aren't those blond curls delightful?' 'What fantastic markings!'
- *When you see someone smile:* 'You've got something to smile about?'
- *If you're in a busy bar:* 'It's very busy in here. I'm surprised because it's not usually like this on a Wednesday.' (Of course it has to be something that's true – no use saying that if it *is* busy on Wednesdays!)
- *When it's sunny:* 'It's so sunny today.'
- *If you've been waiting in a queue for a long time:* 'It's amazing we've been here for so long' *or* 'They've got three tills closed over there' *or* 'They seem to have only one person on at lunchtime.'
- *When someone is having fun:* 'It's great to see someone having fun.'

When picking topics for agreeable chit-chat, go with what's happening right at that moment. The topics should be familiar to the person you're talking to and the statements you make should be easy to agree with.

Use chit-chat as an opportunity to sound out, observe or get a feel for the person you're going to talk to. As their comfort level increases, they will give you more clues as to how they tick. The more you let them chit-chat, the more information you'll get about what they believe, what motivates them and how they do things. Then you will find it much easier to slide in those important questions you want to ask or the vital points you want to make.

Sometimes you can even be a bit naughty and fake it. I was visiting a friend in their flat and met their rather crotchety neighbour on the stairs. She was decorating the midline of the stairwell wall with flowered edging paper. I would never have anything remotely like that in my home, but I recognized that it was her taste. She'd be thinking how much she liked the paper.

I imagined how happy she might feel about it and then said, 'That's nice edging.' She nodded and told me that she'd got the same in her flat and that she loved pale green and pink and that she thought it made the hallways of the apartment block look more like a home and less like anonymous stairwells. And the more she chatted about what she liked, the happier she became.

I knew that one of this woman's pet niggles was to monitor the building. She'd been known to reprimand visitors who'd left their bikes inside the apartment entrance. Which was what I'd just done.

So I said, 'Yes, it's important to have that feeling of being at home. It feels kind of safe. I know you won't mind my leaving my bike there for a while, it's a bit unsafe outside and I know that everyone in this block trusts their neighbours ...'

How could you use chit-chat to lubricate the workings of your life?

Stylish Communication
GIVE 100 PER CENT ATTENTION

One of the biggest challenges for most of us is to give someone 100 per cent attention. Outwardly we may appear to be listening to them, but inside we may be mind reading, jumping to conclusions, rehearsing what to say, filtering, judging or daydreaming. If not reined in, our minds will board any passing express train of thought. Our thoughts will distract us, cloud our minds and block our receptivity to what's going on. Have you ever been listening to someone and found yourself asking, 'Sorry, what was that you said?'

Zen Masters used to come up behind their students and hit them hard on the head. It was to remind them that they weren't present. If they had been, they'd have noticed and been able to take evasive action.

I'm not going to hit you on the head, but here's another way to focus on what's happening to your body.

BODY FOCUS

- Keep your eyes open and focus on the powerpoint area, just below your navel. Keep your attention there.
- Imagine you're aware of what's going on inside your body – how the blood flows and so on.
- Notice your feet and hands.
- As you focus on your body, you will find it's almost impossible to have thoughts.

Paying attention also means being relaxed. You are not thinking about what's going to happen, you are not thinking what has happened, you are just there, in the present, as things *are* happening. That way you get pure information. And you are much more likely to come up with a good response to it.

When you notice you're flying 'away with the fairies', do the body focus exercise above and you'll soon be back giving 100 per cent attention to what's going on around you.

BE WORD-AWARE

Learn to playback people's phrases.

PLAYING BACK PHRASES

- Listen to someone speaking on a video, or video an interview.
- Act as if you're talking to them and playing back their phrases, for example: 'So, Trevor, what you said was that Bush had announced economic sanctions on Zimbabwe.'
- Check back with the video that you've used the correct words in the correct order and not left anything out or added anything in.

This takes practice, but it's a really useful skill.

REMEMBER THE THREE 'A'S OF LISTENING

Julie Soskin, who runs the School of Insight and Intuition, reminded me of her three keys for listening:

1. *Appreciate* the person you are with and focus on the possibilities.
2. Give them your absolute *attention*, be present and enjoy their presence.
3. *Affection* can make a communication go with a real bang and it doesn't have to be sexual. A smile, a friendly wink, a hand on the shoulder or a pat on the arm are all thoughtful, non-threatening and affectionate forms of behaviour that show someone you care and are there for them.

I'm sure you'd agree that it's nice to be appreciated, listened to and given warmth.

FACILITATE AND EMPOWER

Have you ever gone to a friend with your problems and been treated to a whole load of advice? Generally, though, you *aren't* looking to be told what to do, even if you actually ask, 'What should I do?' In these situations, what we *really* want, even if we don't realize it, is for someone to listen to us and to help us to make up our own minds.

Attractive communicators do not dish out advice. They know the conversation is more likely to be a positive one if they encourage the other person to make their own decisions. But they aren't averse to helping them get clear and then throwing in a few subtle suggestions.

When I worked for Henry as a trainer at Happy Computers he taught me the difference between telling someone what to do and allowing them to discover it for themselves. This was a big challenge when helping people to learn something as technical as computer software.

Henry's cardinal rule was: 'Ask, don't tell.' So, instead of telling people what to do, I'd point them to the menu and say something like 'Which menu do you think you'd select to *insert* a *picture?* Look at the menu bar and try it out.' Of course they all got the emphasized words 'insert' and picture' into their heads and felt jolly good as they found it out for themselves.

If they had a question, instead of answering it immediately myself, I'd ask the rest of the group. Often one of them had the right answer.

At other times I'd ask them how they thought they might do a particular thing they'd not yet learned. I'd indicate their manuals and say, 'Why not look it up for yourselves?' Once again they all felt great because they felt as if they'd discovered rather than swallowed the new information. Big difference.

It doesn't matter how many clues and suggestions you give people, as long as they're subtle. If people have a sense that they're making the decision or discovery for themselves, they will feel empowered.

Susan's boyfriend was very chaotic. As she got to know him, it dawned on her that he had all the symptoms of Attention Deficit Disorder. She thought it might be useful for him to realize that he wasn't just a hopeless case, it was actually that his brain was wired differently.

She searched the internet and found a list of characteristics of people who have ADD tendencies. It had been compiled by a reputable MD who was also an ADD person himself. There were about 17 points, each explained in a paragraph with examples. Susan printed it off and handed it to her boyfriend. All she said was, 'Just do me a favour and read through this list. How many of those things seem familiar?'

He ticked off 15 out of 17 points. Then she told him what it meant. She added that most ADD people were considerably more intelligent than average and had the ability to multi-task and that there were ways to cope with it.

Susan knew that it's quite confrontational to diagnose or label people, so she made it easy for her boyfriend to make the discovery for himself.

There's an old tried and tested formula for setting people on the road to discovery: how, what, why, where and when?

Here are some great questions that facilitate self-discovery:

'How do you think you might ...?'

'In what way ...?'

'What do you think could be ...?'

'What difference might that make?'

'Why might ...?'

'Why would that be useful?'

'Where would you like to ...?'

'Where do you believe it comes from?'

'When would be best for you to ...?'

'When might you be able to ...?'

'What would happen if ...?'

Keep this in mind and always look for the route to self-discovery. No one likes a know-it-all, but most people are keen to know it all for themselves!

Of course even the most skilled communicators can't force change on people who aren't ready to change. But everyone can be supportive and use their skills to make another person aware of possibilities and alternatives and be there to encourage them when they are ready.

BOOST THEIR EGO

We all enjoy a good ego boost. And clever communicators know that people are more responsive when they're in a good mood. The gentle art of ego-boosting is a very powerful tool.

Celebrate Good News

Attractive communicators react positively to other people's good news. They also know how to lead people away from gloom towards possibilities. How about you? Do you help people to see through the clouds to the sun?

When attractive communicators spot a good-news boat, they jump on board and join in the celebrations. Superlative words and phrases like 'Wow!', 'Splendid!', 'Excellent!' or 'That's amazing!', 'Well done, you', 'You're so talented, clever, smart ...' roll off their tongues. They are physically expressive and may jump up and down or clap their hands or open their faces wide. They may touch you in some way – patting your back, placing a hand on your shoulder or arm, or even taking your hand and shaking, patting or squeezing it. And whatever they do will be done with a level of energy that matches yours.

Who wouldn't want to have people like that in their life? And what fun it is to be like that. Enthusiasm is a positive emotion that generates lots of immune-boosting chemicals in your body. Makes sense to take a dose of it every day, doesn't it?

If you feel the need to exercise your enthusiasm muscle, here's a simple plan to get you up and running.

ENTHUSIASTIC WORDS

Here are some ways to amplify someone's good feelings.

Hint 1

Make a list of 'enthusiastic' words, the kind of words you say when you're really impressed by something, words like 'Wow!', 'Great!' and 'Fantastic!' Choose ones that suit you and practise saying them with a smile on your face and genuine enthusiasm. Put power and expression into your voice. Go well over the top so that you stretch yourself. When you come to do it for real you won't go as far as that, but you'll find it easy to generate more enthusiasm.

Hint 2

When someone tells you some good news it's your cue to bring out one of your enthusiastic words. Select the word that seems right to you. Put a lot of sound into it. Don't be afraid to let rip. Be bold and loud! Fizzle and sparkle! Imagine you can see the word written out in bold in a colour that you love with lots of exclamation marks after it.

Hint 3

Add the word into a sentence which more or less repeats what it is that the person is so pleased about. If, for example, they've just told you they passed their driving test after four attempts, say something like 'Wow, you must be really pleased that *after all those attempts you finally made it!'*

Hint 4

If you can, touch them reassuringly and say something like 'I'm impressed' or 'How do you do it?' or 'You have every right to feel proud/excited/pleased.' By doing this you are giving them permission to feel good and celebrate themselves in the presence of another person – you!

Touching them at the same time as uttering a uplifting celebratory phrase has the delicious side-effect of linking their excitement to your words and touch.

Hint 5

Get them to tell you about the experience. Ask questions that lead them to focus on the good bits. 'What was the best moment?' 'What did it feel like when you found out?' Be excited and you will amplify their own good feelings.

Hint 6

Pat them on the back or squeeze their hand or clap your hands and say once again (using your own words), 'Well done, that's great news!' You'll leave them feeling on top of the world and feeling very positive towards you.

After Sammi failed her driving test three times, she called me in tears. 'I'm a failure!' she wailed. 'No, *you're* not a failure,' I said. 'You *failed your test* – and haven't you heard that saying *"Fourth time lucky"?'*

Sammi had taken her behaviour and turned it into part of her identity. Dangerous. Fortunately, changing the standard 'third time lucky' phrase to suit her situation made her laugh and shocked her out of it! People will always have their off-moments and sometimes just a word or two can shift their focus and uplift them.

When people start to go into their problems, make a point of focusing on what's good about them and get them to think of past examples that refute what they're claiming and lead them to possibilities. Here are some examples to give you the idea. You can adapt them to suit your own style.

- *'Everything seems to be going wrong for me.'* Get them to focus on a positive achievement and use it as a reminder that they *can* make things go right: 'But sometimes things do go right for you. I remember how you ...'
- *'I just can't seem to get focused.'* Remind them of times when they were focused and apply it to their current situation: 'How about when you play tennis? You really seem focused then. What do you do to get so focused?'
- *'I just don't think I'm going to be able to afford it.'* Get them to focus on what they have to do to get past this block: 'What would you need to have happen so you could afford it?'
- *'I'm pretty useless at paying compliments.'* Tell them about a time someone paid you a compliment and how good it made you feel. Get them to focus on what they like about particular people: 'You've got some good friends and people you love, haven't you? Tell me why you like them. What else do you value in them? How have they helped you?'
- *'I'm too quiet/short/whatever.'* Get them to focus on the positive aspects of what they see as a negative trait: 'Sometimes silence can be more powerful than talking for the sake of it.' 'You're not short, you're petite.' 'Tom Cruise is pretty short/Carrie from *Sex and the City* is tiny but oozes sex appeal.'

REFOCUSING STATEMENTS

Make a list of negative sentences similar to those above and come up with as many positive refocusing statements as you can. Don't censor what comes up – even if the statements sound ridiculous, you will be giving your positive focus muscle a great workout!

Of course, though, it's wise to remember that sometimes people just aren't ready to change and you can't be the world's therapist. If people are determined to whine and moan, removing yourself from their company is a desirable option. Why hang around with someone who's spreading doom and gloom? You might catch it too!

CHARISMATIC COMMUNICATION 102: LINGUISTIC WIZARDRY

Linguist wizards know that well-crafted language can work magic. Wouldn't you like to know what they know and how they do what they do?

Patterns of Communication

Communication doesn't just formulate itself out of thin air. It's generated from who we are and what's going on for us at that moment. And when it comes to making sense of the world, we aren't consciously aware of every bit of raw data. We have filters operating.

Our filters determine what comes into our awareness and what stays outside it. A filter is like a computer programme that runs in the background, sorting for specific information and generating relevant behaviour patterns. It generates beliefs, values, criteria for judgement and strategies, all of which drive us to do certain things in certain ways:

We have beliefs about ourselves, other people and the way the world is. **These beliefs are generated from people and events around us and our own experience of life.**

We have values. **Certain things are important to us. And some are more important than others. We are drawn to people whose values match ours and we judge people by our own values.**

We use strategies that we have developed for dealing with life. **Strategies are a series of activities that we carry out in a specific way in order to get what we want.**

We have criteria by which we gauge things.

Here are some ways in which all of the above come into play:

- Let's say you have a belief that all fat people are jolly. When you meet a fat person, you will remember all the moments when they laugh or smile and ignore the times when they don't.
- Maybe you think freedom is one of the most important things in your life. If you meet someone who works 9 to 5 and you associate that with lack of freedom, you'll probably feel sorry for them. But what if their biggest value

is security and working in an office gives them freedom from worrying about where the next penny will come from?

- If you wanted to sell something to someone, wouldn't it help if you knew what was important to them and could relate your product to them in those terms?
- Two people are not happy in their jobs. They decide to make a change. The first person leaves because they are excited about all the benefits of the new job. The second person makes the change because there are just too many things they hate about their current job. Would it be wise to use the same motivation strategy with person one as you would with person two?
- Success for one person may be getting a job and for another it might be building a multi-million dollar business. One person might think that being sexually liberated means having had more than six partners, to another it might mean an open relationship, exploring the furthest reaches of sexuality. Wouldn't it be useful to know what people mean by words before you jump to conclusions?

When you are privy to what people believe, what's important to them, how they go about their life or the way in which they make judgements, you have all you need to create exquisitely tailored and charismatic communication. And when you get good at this, you can do it anywhere, anytime and with anyone. It's invaluable when you are trying to sell something or persuade someone or make love to them. Best of all, people will love being around you and will let you into their world. They will feel good because you 'get' them.

Most people act according to a variety of imprinted patterns of behaviour.

People's patterns are the keys to what motivates and influences them and how they make decisions. They are recognizable from the specific language people use. Great communicators are very alert to patterns. They are skilled at recognizing and decoding what others say. As your own pattern mastery develops, you will be amazed at the power and possibilities of your communication and how effortlessly you are able to negotiate, sell, influence and attract.

So what are you looking for? Here are specific patterns that people commonly bring into play. As you read them through, think about yourself and how you react. You'll find out heaps about yourself too!

CRITERIA

> Criteria are those factors that must take place, or be promised
> or believed, in order for someone to take action. Ultimately, they
> show you the precise path that you need to follow in order to
> gather from your client exactly *why* they buy.
>
> **Kendrick Cleveland**

Ultimately, whether we're buying or sizing up a new job or someone for a relationship or friendship, we're driven by our criteria. Our criteria are our personal signposts to satisfaction. How do you know what someone's criteria are? It pays to do a little detective work.

If you're going out on a date with someone new, for example, and you're going to a restaurant, it might seem courteous to ask where they'd like to eat, but if they are reluctant to impose their choice on you it may seem like pressure. A direct question can be uncomfortable for someone who takes time to open up.

On the other hand, if you just plan a surprise, it could go horribly wrong. A friend of mine was asked out to dinner by a new date and discovered to her horror that he'd booked them into the trendiest Chinese restaurant in town. What he didn't know was that my friend is allergic to monosodium glutamate, an additive which is integral to most Chinese food. She was faced with the embarrassment of having to ask the waiter if they used MSG. They did and there was virtually nothing she could eat on the menu. She had to ask them to prepare something special for her. Even though they willingly did so, she was put in an awkward situation and felt guilty because her new date had gone to so much trouble.

If only he'd taken the time to do a little research. All it takes is a few simple questions. Not only will they give you more information, but your interest will make the other person feel *valued*! You can adapt the following questions for your own purposes:

'What kinds of things do you like to do on an evening out?'
'What kind of things do you look for when you eat out?'
'What's the best restaurant you've ever been to? What makes it so good?'
'What's your worst experience of eating out?'

'What are absolute no-nos for you in a restaurant?'

'What was your most favourite experience of eating out and what made it special?'

'How did you feel about it?'

If they give you several reasons why they like something, ask them: 'If you could have just one thing, what would it be? What next? What next?' That will build up a list of their criteria, and in order of importance.

Notice whether they're coming up with what they like or what they don't like. That will give you an insight into their motivational strategies.

When you've built up an idea of what's most important to them, you can compare it to what you enjoy and make up your mind to do something that meets both your criteria.

MOTIVATION

Everyone gets motivated in different ways. What about you? If you have ever left a job, what made you go? Was it because it got so bad you couldn't stand it? Politics, having your actions questioned, too much stress, working 24/7, pressure to perform, competition, being held back, being bored? Or was it because you dreamt about doing something else, working for another company, getting more money, more satisfaction, working for yourself, having freedom to choose your hours, more self-expression, more respect, more autonomy, more spare time?

Which of the above do you relate to more? You just got an insight into one of your patterns.

GO FOR IT OR WAIT FOR IT?

Do you initiate situations and sometimes jump in feet first, or do you prefer to wait for the right moment or for someone else to make the first move?

Jim is known in his social circle as 'action man'. He's quick to approach strangers and chat up women. He can be found organizing his friends into doing things. If he sees an opportunity, he rarely lets it pass by. He takes the shortest route to his goals even if it's not necessarily the wisest one. He makes up his mind in an instant. Sometimes he's accused of being too pushy. He tends to speak quickly, and might fidget and appear impatient. He isn't very good at sitting around for a long time.

When someone has a 'go for it' pattern in place, they sound very much in control and use the active tense, which they personalize: '*I* am going to the party.' '*I* believe that this is the case.' Sometimes they come across a bit strong. They make up their minds quickly and often say things like 'Let's go' or 'Come on, gang.'

If you were going to influence someone who was very 'go for it', you would speak quickly and energetically to give them a sense of impending action and would use words like:

'Go for it!'
'Why wait?'
'Run with it.'
'Let's go, right now.'

> Marla stands on the edge of a party waiting to be introduced to someone or for someone to approach her. If she sees something she likes in a shop, she'll make several visits before she makes up her mind. Her friends see her as laid back. They expect her to go along with most things, and she generally does.

People who are in 'wait for it' mode tend to use the passive tense a lot more. They give responsibility to someone else:

'I've been invited to a party.'
'People say that that's the case.'
'My friends tell me I'm ...'

They wait for someone else to take action or may spend a lot of time weighing up the pros and cons of a situation:

'I suppose I could if ...'
'Let me think about it.'

They take a lot of convincing and like to analyse things:

'Maybe we could ...'
'I'm not quite sure.'

If you wanted to relate well to their way of doing things you would use words like:

'Take your time to think about it.'
'What do you need to know?'
'Consider this ...'
'Think about it this way ...'

Give them the facts and time they need to make up their mind.

A great question to check out whether someone is 'go for it' or 'wait for it' is: 'How would you react if you were presented with the opportunity to work abroad?' Jim might get quite excited and say something like 'Wow! What a great idea!' Even if he doesn't have any information about where or when, he's already painting his own picture of the country and the job he'd be doing. Marla would probably say, 'I don't know, it would depend.' She couldn't possibly get excited about something without knowing all the facts.

TOWARDS PLEASURE OR AWAY FROM PAIN?

Are you motivated towards something you want or are you more turned on by the thought of escaping a situation?

> Rob had problems meeting his deadlines. I asked him what it was that made him get up finally and start to write. He replied, 'When the pressure gets really bad, I get going.' When Rob gets the first little voice saying, 'That piece is due soon,' he just puts it away. As he moves closer to the deadline the voices get louder and the feelings more painful. It's not until the pain gets really bad that he is pushed to run away from it. And it's only then that he can start writing. Rob often talks about problems and about getting away from things. His language is very 'escapist'. When he's talking, he often shakes his head or moves his hands in a pushing or brushing away motion.

■ ■ ■

> Lucy jogs at least three times a week, even when the weather is bad. I asked what got her out of bed and on the run. She told me that she lay in bed and thought of how good she was going to feel when she'd finished her run and

of the fit body that she was building. Lucy tends to talk about goals and what she can gain or have. She does a lot of nodding and pointing or gesturing in front of her.

When it comes to motivational direction, Rob and Lucy have two very different patterns. Rob acts when he feels the urgent need to move *away from* pain and Lucy moves *towards* pleasure.

If you were going to trigger Rob into action, you would use language that focused on what he wanted to escape or prevent:

'Now you won't have to do ... any more.'
'You can prevent ... happening by doing ...'
'Here's a way you can get rid of ...'
'If you don't have ..., you won't get ...'

Emphasize how doing something can get him away from something else and make him more aware of the unwanted results he'll get when he *doesn't* do something. He will most likely respond to requests to find out what's wrong. He will also be easily distracted. To give himself more balance, he may need to focus on what he can achieve.

Some people might say that Rob's way is not the most useful or pleasant, but it's a strategy that works for many. Societies for the prevention of cruelty towards animals and children often focus on the pain because it's a great motivator.

On the other hand, Lucy will get turned on by all the wonderful things she can expect when she's done something. To motivate her, you would use language like:

'What will happen when you get ...?'
'These are the benefits ...'
'Here's what you would achieve ...'
'Won't it be ... when you do ...?'

Lucy will look for what works or what is possible. To keep her feet on the ground, she may need to be reminded from time to time about what can go wrong.

About 40 per cent of people tend to be pain-avoiders and 40 per cent pleasure-seekers. The remaining 20 per cent are a mixture of both.

If you want to find out someone's motivational direction, ask them to think of a big change they made – perhaps buying a place to live, moving to another country or changing jobs or partners. Ask them: 'When you changed ..., what did it do for you?'

Notice whether they tell you about all the things they gained or whether they sigh with relief at all the things they escaped from.

As I was writing this I heard this on a house-buying programme on TV:

'Give me a picture of your ideal house.'
'I don't want one of those little country cottage-type things where you have to stoop to go through doors with small dark windows. So I think those listed buildings are out for us.'
'So what else is on the essential list?'
'I want to have a kitchen with access to the garden so the children don't bring their muddy shoes through the house.'

In order to find out what she *does* want, this woman has first to check what she *doesn't* want. In order to get someone like this to decide what they want, you have to let them go through this process and then ask them: 'So if you don't want that, what *would* be right for you?'

When you know whether a person is drawn to something or trying to move away from something, it's a major communication breakthrough. You can modify your language to match theirs and they will start thinking, 'Mmmmm, this person really understands what I want. This person is so like *me*.' Then they're bound to find you more attractive and to be more open to whatever you have to say.

'I'M OK' V. 'AM I OK?'

Are you a self-starter who knows what's right for you or do you need outside influence to help you make up your mind?

Dylan is a graphic designer. He knows when he's done a good job. He doesn't need someone else to tell him so. In fact he rarely asks anyone else's advice and doesn't take easily to being told what to do. When his boss gives him feedback on his work, which isn't always 100 per cent perfect, instead of asking what he could do better, he's more likely to assume his boss hasn't got a clue and question his judgement. Dylan judges things by his own standards. If someone gives him instructions, he tends to think of them simply as information which he can use to make a decision for himself. He tends to say 'I know' a lot.

If you were chatting to Dylan, you'd notice how contained he appeared, with minimal gestures and facial expressions.

If you wanted to have an influential conversation with him, you might say things like:

'Well, of course you're the one who has to decide.'
'Why not give it a try and let me know what you think?'
'Here are all the facts. Have a think about it and let me know what you want to do.'

Make sure you give him enough information so that he can make his own decision. You won't persuade someone like Dylan by telling him what other people think.

Larry hasn't a clue about clothes and always asks his wife what he should wear when they go out. When he hands in a report to his boss, he's never 100 per cent sure it's right until his boss tells him so. In conversation Larry often shrugs his shoulders, leans forward and raises his eyebrows in that 'Is that OK?' look. He says things like 'I'm not sure if that's what you wanted' or 'I couldn't decide what was the best way to approach this.'

If you wanted to get Larry on your side, you would give him references and expert opinions:

'Mary really loved the play.'
'Everyone at our gym wants to join the Pilates class.'
'It's a New York Times bestseller.'

Tell him how much other people will be impressed or what an impact he might have. Don't leave the Larrys of this world to make up their own minds.

If you want to know whether someone is self-referenced or more reliant on external opinions, just ask them:

'How did you know you did that well?'
'How did you know that was right for you?'
'If you'd done something you thought was pretty good, how would you react if someone gave you negative criticism?'

The split between self-referenced and other-referenced motivation traits is about 40 per cent self-motivated and 40 per cent reliant on others, with the remaining 20 per cent being a mixture of both.

CHOICES V. STEP BY STEP

Are you a possibility-seeker who is always looking for new ways to do something or do you prefer to follow a procedure?

Nick and Suzy have been married for six years. They are very different and the way they've learned to get on together is to understand, respect and work with each other's foibles.

Nick's favourite saying is 'If it ain't broke, don't fix it.' When he cooks, he always follows a recipe to the letter. He's fantastic at putting together self-assembly furniture. He takes out every piece, checks that they're all there and follows the instructions to the letter. If he gets a new 'toy' he always pores over the manual before he starts fiddling with the controls. When he learned to ski, he was meticulous about taking lessons and he even read books on the subject as well as making sure he followed every word his instructor uttered.

Suzy is very different. She gets ideas for new projects and rushes in enthusiastically, but she soon gets bored and is on to the next thing. If you wanted someone to see something through from beginning to end, Suzy wouldn't be the best choice! When she cooks, she looks at a recipe or two for the same thing, closes the book and does her own thing. Nick laughingly complains that he never gets the same dish twice. Suzy hates being pinned down and often has several plans ready to put into action. She sometimes finds it difficult to make a decision because it might mean she loses out on something. And above all, she loves to break the rules!

If you wanted to influence someone like Nick, you would talk about something being the 'right way' or being 'tried and tested'. If you wanted him to get a task done, you would give him a step-by-step procedure: 'First do X, then Y and finally Z.' Nick would also be more likely to buy something if you were to give him a start-to-finish process: 'First you can look at the car, then you can have a test drive and then we'll discuss finance and you can drive it away.'

If you wanted to get on well with Suzy, on the other hand, you would talk about opportunity and choice and breaking the rules and would give her alternatives. If you were selling to her, you would tell her, 'There's got to be a way to find what's right for you.' If she couldn't make up her mind between two items, you would show her a way she could have both: 'Why not take both?' or 'You could take this one now and come back for the other one next week.' If you are dating someone like Suzy, be sure to come up with lots of different ideas for things to do, places to go and food to eat. Variety and masses of choice are the spice of Suzy's life.

To find out whether you are a 'choices' or 'step-by-step' person, a good question to ask yourself is: 'Why did you choose your present partner/home/job?'

When I asked Suzy why she married Nick, she gave me a long list of reasons. 'Oh he was so handsome, and he makes me laugh, and we have so much fun, and he loved skiing, and we both wanted children, and, and, and ...'

When I asked Nick why he married Suzy, he didn't give me any reasons *why* but told me *how* it had come about: 'We met each other at school and then we dated for a few years and marriage just seemed like the natural conclusion.'

SAME V. DIFFERENT

Do you like things to stay the same for years on end? Maybe you don't mind some change as long as it's not too drastic? Or are you the sort of person who thrives on constant and radical shifts? Or are you happy with radical change but also comfortable in a situation that is growing or evolving?

'Same'-oriented people say things like 'You're with us or against us' – they want you to declare your similarity or difference – or 'If it ain't broke, don't fix it' – they don't see the need to mess with something that is OK as it is. They always tend to choose the same things on the menu.

'Different'-type people say things like 'I wonder if we could improve on this' – even if something works, they can't help wanting to alter it. They always like to try new things. 'Same' people follow recipes to the letter and 'different' people add their own touches or make up their own recipes.

If you wanted to motivate someone who likes things to stay the same, you would point out similarities:

'It's just like ...'
'He reminds me of ...'
'You'll be familiar with this.'
'You'll like her because she's very similar to ...'
'Alligator tastes just like chicken.'
'When they used that system it really worked for them.'

If you wanted to encourage someone who likes things to change, point out the differences:

'The great thing about this company is that we're pushing the boundaries.'
'He's just the opposite of your ex.'
'You'll love this restaurant – it's a totally new concept in eating.'
'Alligator – it tastes like nothing you've ever tried.'
'No one's done that yet, you could be on to a winner.'

MATCH V. MISMATCH

How do you respond to being told what to do? Is your immediate response to comply or do you always challenge such demands or refuse them?

> Jillian didn't like being told what to do. When her boyfriend told her to pack a bag and meet him at the airport, she said to him, 'Why didn't you ask me if I wanted to go away this weekend?' She later admitted to me that she loved to go away for weekends but she resented her boyfriend making plans for her. She said she even got annoyed when he said things like 'Let's go to the Thai restaurant tonight.' 'No' is a big feature in Jillian's vocabulary – sometimes even when she's in agreement!

People who mismatch like Jillian often play the Devil's Advocate. It sometimes seems as if they disagree with everything you say. They ask loads of questions, use the word 'but' often and will frequently interrupt.

If you want to get along with a mismatcher, do *not* tell them what to do. Instead always ask them what they *want* to do, *how* they want to do it, *when* and *where*. You can also use reverse psychology. Say things like:

> **'Well, you may disagree with this, but ...'**
> **'You probably won't want to do this, although ...'**
> **'I suspect you won't like ...'**

Notice how the words like 'probably' 'may' and 'suspect' leave it a bit open. This way the person will pick up on the point you're making without feeling 'directed' and they won't be able to resist mismatching:

> **'I *will* agree ...'**
> **'How do you know I don't want to do it?'**
> **'I *do* like it.'**

If you're a bit of a mismatcher yourself, make it easier on people – make a joke of your perennial disagreement. Lizzie told me how once a friend of hers had said, 'You always disagree with me,' to which she had replied, 'No, I don't!' Practise agreeing sometimes and doing something someone tells you to do just for the fun of it.

BIG PICTURE V. DETAIL

Do you just like to get a broad overview of something or do you thrive on lots of detail?

I'm more of a big-picture person. You can enthuse me with a concept, but when you start getting into detail, my mind boggles. If I'm getting too much detail, I often say things like 'Get to the point' or 'What's the overall idea?'

'Big chunkers' like me are more inclined to give overviews or summaries than go into great detail. We process things quickly and tend to talk more quickly than average. We process information in big chunks, concepts and abstracts. And we react well when people present things in this way to us. And when I communicate with a 'detailed' person, I have to pay attention to how I do it, just as a detailed person should with me.

If you want to persuade someone like me to do something or you are trying to sell me something, paint a broad picture, make it snappy and stay away from detail. Generally big chunkers don't mind detail if it comes later, but if it comes too soon, it can cloud their initial reaction. So use phrases like:

'I've got this great idea ...'
'Broadly speaking ...'
'The overall idea is ...'
'The main point I want to make is ...'
'In principle, what do you think?'

My partner, on the other hand, is Mr Specific. He likes information in small chunks. He is very conscientious about detail. He's a journalist and often produces double the amount of words he's been commissioned to write because he keeps adding *more* detail. He has difficulty prioritizing because he can get bogged down in detail, but his ability to notice everything makes him a fantastic proofreader! He takes much more time than I do to process information, so I make sure we don't go to Chinese restaurants with endlessly long menus!

If you want to get on with someone like my partner, include plenty of detail in your conversation and speak quite slowly. Give them time to process the information. If you are trying to sell them something, be prepared to provide a lot of information and don't expect them to make up their minds right away. Use words like 'precisely' and 'specifically' and gain rapport with their way of thinking by saying things like 'Is there anything else you need to make up your mind?' or 'I know you'll want to take a little time to mull over the facts before you decide.'

It's easy to spot a big chunker from a detail merchant. Ask someone to describe a recent holiday or how they spent their day at work and notice how much detail they go into. Around 60 per cent of people are big-picture oriented. Only 15 per cent of people are detail merchants and about 25 per cent are a mixture of both.

UNEMOTIONAL V. EMOTIONAL

How tuned in are you to other people's behaviour? Do you pay attention to what they say and miss what they are doing or are you sensitive to their body language as well? Do you pick up on their emotions? Do they show any?

> Kevin rarely shows his emotions. When he's chatting to someone he doesn't make those little agreeable noises that most of us like and he rarely nods. He doesn't seem to know when other people might be feeling emotional and will go strictly by what they say. If you tell Kevin you're fine, even in a pretty sour voice, he'll assume you *are* fine!
>
> Once when Kevin was chatting to a rather fat woman he asked her if it was hormonal. He was simply intrigued as to why some people are overweight and he had no idea that he'd insulted her! Kevin is not a people person, which is why he is very happy in his job as a computer programmer. And it's also why he has such a hard time meeting women.

People like Kevin are often quite slow to respond. The first thing they focus on is the content of what you're saying. They pay little attention to your emotional signals, such as voice tone, gestures and body language, and tend to seek out the kind of jobs where communication skills aren't essential. And if they're focused on reading or watching TV, they rarely hear what you're saying

When communicating with someone like Kevin, concentrate on content. Take care with the *words* that you use to convey your feelings, but don't expect them to react to any emotional *signals*. There's no point in sulking with these people because they just won't get it. Just do your best to make your point logically, otherwise they'll pick holes in it. If you're preparing a proposal for them, keep out the emotional content. They want to know how and if it's going to work, not whether people are going to be happy.

> My friend Pammie, on the other hand, is very receptive to other people's emotions. If someone is unhappy, she feels for them. You can't fool her with slick words, because she reads what's behind them. She's particularly good at making people feel comfortable. When she listens to you she makes appropriate agreeable sounds and you feel as if you've been heard. That's

why she's such a sought-after celebrity interviewer. She turns on her tape and concentrates on the other person. People openly tell her things, even though she's a journalist, because they feel as if she's in tune with them and because she genuinely cares.

People like Pammie pick up on the emotional content of a conversation and adjust accordingly. They make frequent eye contact and become livelier in the presence of others and they pay attention to the way you are saying things.

If you want to communicate with someone like Pammie, use lots of friendly gestures, smile a lot and make eye contact. When writing e-mails to her, spice them up by with plenty of emoticons, otherwise they may seem too impersonal to her.

Thank goodness the majority of people tend to be more like Pammie than Kevin! But that's probably because I'm such a people person myself.

DECISIONS, DECISIONS ...

What's the best way to convince you to take a job, buy something or to go out with someone? How do you learn? Do you prefer it when someone shows you something or do you like them to tell you about it or to have a discussion with them? Do you like to read up on a topic or product before you commit? Or do you have to get in there and try it for yourself? Might it be different depending on the situation?

When you're trying to sell something to someone or get them to agree to take action, it's useful to know how they process information. Most of us have a preferred sense. When you communicate with someone via the sense they favour, your communication will double its attraction factor.

'Show Me'

Liam needs to see a product before he buys. He is more likely to purchase things via mail order if he can at least see an illustration of what he's buying. A diagram or some kind of visual material will always help him decide.

'Show me' people are particularly good at picking up signals and body language, which means it's harder to fool them with words. They tend to use words that are visually oriented. And they tend to talk and process information quickly. So if you are describing something to a 'show me' person, make sure you paint a really good picture. Talk about colours, shade, shape, light and appearance, the vision. Make them comfortable by using visual words and phrases like:

see	colourful	Picture it.	Let me paint you
show	visualize	Take a look at it.	a picture.
look	imagine	Let me show you.	
diagram	clarify	Does this look	
perceive	throw light on	good?	

Can you visualize that?

Where possible, use more pictures and fewer words. If you're giving directions, draw a map and give plenty of visual landmarks. 'Show me' people often struggle with written instructions, so keep your phrases short, efficient and accurate.

'Tell Me'

Lindsay responds to being told things. She always did well at school because most of the teaching was oral.

If you wanted to sell to or persuade Lindsay, you'd have much more success if you were to tell her everything she needed to know.

'Tell me' people will use more auditory words and phrases. They are naturally good listeners. They may be OK with e-mails, but often their favourite medium is the telephone. They are easily distracted by noises going on around them, so if you want to get your message across, find somewhere peaceful to chat to them. They often have a good vocabulary and are picky about the meaning of words, so you'd be wise to choose yours carefully. They will be particularly impressed if you repeat their phrases back to them accurately.

When you talk to them, concentrate on auditory words and phrases such as:

hear	rhythm	Sounds good?	Does that click?
talk	harmonious	Let me tell you	Tell me what you
listen	Does that	all about it.	want, I'm
question	resonate with	I can hear that you	listening.
dialogue	you?	are interested.	

Let's discuss this.

'Give Me Facts

> Darryl really responds well to written material. If you called him on the phone you wouldn't get much out of him, but you would get on his right side by offering to put it all in writing, either by letter or e-mail. And he'd enjoy plenty of facts and figures to mull over.

People like Darryl crave data. If you are giving them directions, put in as much detail as possible and put it in writing!

Most 'fact hungry' people will still have a preference for one of the other channels, but those who don't often appear somewhat robotic and unemotional, like Data in *Star Trek*. Once you've got an idea of what sense works best for them, use it, but you will boost your chances of a result if you give them the additional comfort of written information.

'Let Me Try It'

> Caron finds it really hard to make up her mind about anything unless she's tried it out. Her mate Tim wanted her to go on a personal development course that had really helped him. He told her about it enthusiastically and showed her stuff on the internet, and she admitted how much he'd changed for the better, but she still didn't sign up until he took her on an introductory evening. She had to experience it for herself before she was convinced.

If you wanted to persuade someone like Caron to buy a product or try an activity, you'd be wise to let her have a go. If a salesperson emphasizes the looks of a car or talks endlessly he may find her unresponsive. But if he asks her if she wants to get a feel for the car by sitting in it, touching the upholstery and then driving it, he's really upped his chances of getting a sale. And while you're about it, 'let me try it' people respond well to appropriate touch. So make sure you give them a warm handshake. They tend to speak more slowly and take longer to process information. Give them time for it to sink in. They're checking everything you say with how they 'feel' about it.

They respond well to touchy-feely words and phrases like:

feel	grapple	Let's get to grips with this.	Try it out for yourself.
touch	warm		
hot	grasp	This will give you a good feel for what I mean.	Have a go.
cold			

Remember that not everyone who exhibits signs of a pattern will *always* behave like that. We may adopt one pattern in one situation and another in a different situation. And we will definitely exhibit a mixture of patterns. So beware of labelling people. It's always wise to assess what pattern they are using at a particular time rather than relying on how they behaved in another situation.

Wordpower
MEANINGFUL WORDS

> 'When I use a word,' Humpty Dumpty said, in a rather scornful tone,
> 'it means just what I choose it to mean – neither more nor less.'
>
> **Lewis Carroll, *Through the Looking Glass***

Some words are what I call 'big emotion' words – words like 'love', 'monogamy', 'trust', 'confidence', 'happiness', 'success', 'fulfilment' and 'acceptance'. These words have meaning beyond the dictionary definitions. We all have unique meanings for those words, and mine won't be the same as yours. If you want to prove it to yourself, try this exploration.

BIG EMOTIONS

- Get a group of friends together and think of two or three 'big emotion' words.
- Ask them to write down five words that first come to mind with when they hear or see those words. Make sure they don't edit or censor, but just write down what comes up first.
- Compare your words.

I'm willing to bet that there will be a lot of different words and maybe only one or two in common.

In any form of communication, always have in mind that what *you* mean by a word or phrase isn't necessarily what another person means. You can save yourself a lot of trouble by asking a clarifying question:

'What do you mean by ...?'
'Could you explain ... a little more?'
'Can you elaborate on ...?'

EMPOWERING V. DISABLING LANGUAGE

There are certain words that we use nowadays because they make people feel better. What comes to mind when you think of a 'garbage collector'? Or a 'refuse disposal operative'?

What's the difference between thinking of someone as 'disabled' and thinking of them as 'challenged'? The use of the word 'challenge' makes a lot of difference. 'Disabled' doesn't hold out hope, but a 'challenge' is something that can be conquered. Challenge has possibility.

Language can literally affect the way we feel and influence our general outlook on life. The more we use disabling language, the more disabled we're going to feel. When we make a point of saucing up our language with empowering words and phrases, we feel empowered and hopeful. Which is more attractive to you?

Look out for phrases like the ones below. As you read through them, notice the thoughts that come to mind and the feelings that you are getting in your body.

'I'm stressed out.'
'I've got so many problems.'
'I'm in the middle of a crisis.'
'It's a nightmare.'
'I'm on a deadline.'
'It's really urgent.'
'I'm under threat of redundancy.'
'It's all going wrong.'
'I'm stuck.'
'I'm completely bogged down.'

How often do you use these phrases? Pay attention to people who use them often. Are they great to be around or do they stress *you* out?

Even worse, sometimes people seem to thrive on this.

> Miranda has worked wonders in her life, but it's always been when she's really up against it and she's pushed herself so far financially and mentally that she has to come up with a very creative solution in a short space of time. She admits that it's quite a painful process and that she doesn't feel good physically when she's stressed out. But chaos, nightmares, crises and panic get her going.

What people like Miranda don't realize is that they are being driven by fear. This releases adrenalin, which puts a lot of stress on their internal organs, particularly the kidneys. It is *not* healthy to think like this too often.

Miranda is learning that with a bit of effort she can change her focus and learn from the attitude of people like Ray.

> Ray is what I call a 'challenger'. His lifestyle is poles apart from Miranda's. Ray really knows what he wants out of life. He has a sense of purpose and believes that when he's on the right track anything is possible.

> Ray says things like:

> 'It's a real challenge.'
> 'I'm on the verge of a breakthrough.'
> 'There's light at the end of the tunnel.'
> 'Tomorrow's another day.'
> 'I've done my best.'
> 'It will all work out perfectly.'
> 'The turning-point is in sight.'
> 'This is a great opportunity.'
> 'Things are evolving.'
> 'I can choose from several strategies.'
> 'I know success is just around the corner.'
> 'The possibilities are endless.'

How do you feel when you read through those phrases? Need I say more? Would you rather live on the edge of a crisis like Miranda or on the verge of a breakthrough like Ray?

Brush up on your empowering language! That's an order, but you can take it as a strong suggestion and know that you have choice!

Think about the effect you will have on people when you use empowering language. See yourself smiling, hear yourself saying those words in an uplifting voice tone … and then feel the nice feelings.

Make a note of the words and phrases you use most frequently. If any disabling words or phrases slip into your everyday language, come up with an empowering word to use instead. A 'near impossible task', for example, becomes 'something that will challenge your abilities or stretch your imagination'.

It doesn't matter if you drop a disabling word clanger when you're talking to someone – just make the switch. The other person will reap the benefits of your empowering language and it will make them forget what you said before. You can even make a joke of it: 'Oops! I think I'm going to take that back and try again. I'm trying to use more empowering language because it makes people feel better, doesn't it?' Smile and put up your hands and say something like 'Mistakes are good for me. I'm learning.' People always like it if you show you're willing to learn from your mistakes.

Once you start talking to yourself in empowering language, you'll find yourself using it much more naturally with others anyway.

LUSCIOUS WORDS

I was reading the blurb on the back of a pack of fruit salad. It said: 'Each fruit has been selected for its **lusciousness**.' The word 'lusciousness' had been printed in bigger and bolder type than the rest of the sentence. As I read it I heard myself say, '*Luscious*,' in a stronger, sexier tone. It conjured up all kinds of images.

Words like 'luscious' are very powerful. I can't think of one negative connotation for luscious. It's the same with 'delightful'. It's pure delight!

What luscious words can you use to sweeten your language?

> delightful, luscious, sensual, charming, pleasant, lovely,
> wonderful, enjoyable, amusing, magnificent, superb,

breathtaking, amazing, grand, splendid, tremendous, impressive, marvellous, scrumptious, fabulous, super, moving, noticeable, outstanding, wicked, tremendous, awesome, remarkable, extraordinary, astounding, significant, incredible, astonishing, terrific, stupendous, dazzling, alluring, stunning, eye catching, spectacular, striking, awe-inspiring, excellent …

I used the thesaurus on my computer to come up with those words, and as I was doing it, all the associations with those words sparked off and I noticed how high I was beginning to feel. Luscious.

See if you can come up with some luscious words of your own.

YOUR LUSCIOUS WORDS DAY

- Pick a day to be your Luscious Words Day.
- Resolve to put out as many luscious words as are appropriate.
- Whenever you hear yourself saying, 'That's *nice,*' immediately ask, 'What luscious word could I use in its place?' And use it. You'll soon notice the difference.

Enrich your 'luscious' words vocabulary and you'll bring lots of sunshine into people's lives.

CONTROLLING LANGUAGE

We know that our choice of language can have a powerful effect on us. Never more so when we use 'controlling' language.

Are you using words that suggest that something will definitely happen?

'I simply must have/do …'
'There's no question that …'
'I haven't got a choice.'
'It's in the stars.'
'It's inevitable/unavoidable/predestined.'
'It's bound to …'
'I'm destined to …'

These words reflect a powerful belief about how things will turn out. This can be empowering or limiting. If you are going for a job and you know it's the job for you, it's very empowering to say, 'There's no question that I'm the one for this job.' But if you are going for a job and say, 'There's no chance I'll get this job,' that's pretty limiting.

So be careful how you use these words. Try to use them only with positive connotations. If you feel negative about something, say to yourself, 'It might turn out like that, but I can't really know.' And then ask yourself:

'What would it be like if it wasn't like that?'
'What would it be like if it was like [what you want]?'
'What would have to happen?'

You can use these questions with other people too when you notice them using negatively limiting language.

Some people use what I call 'not quite there yet' language. There is something they want, but at the same time they are putting it out of their control, allowing fate or circumstances to take over. And sometimes they just put off deciding or push it to the back of their minds. Watch out for words like:

'I ought to, but ...'
'I'd like to, but ...'
'I would if I could.'
'It might be possible.'
'Maybe ...'
'Who knows?'
'Perhaps ...'
'I'm not sure ...'
'I'd have to think about it ...'

Isn't it interesting that the word that seems to fit most naturally after many of these phrases is 'but'? More on this later.

■ ■ ■

Noticing people's language patterns and the context in which they use them will open the doors to their minds, allowing you to slip in quietly and effectively.

And now, let me tell you a story …

THE POWER OF STORYTELLING

Don't you just love a good story – the kind that draws you in and keeps you spellbound? Storytelling is a powerful way to effect change on people. As they listen to the story, the deeper meaning just sinks in.

Here are a couple of everyday situations where stories work better than anything.

Who I Am

> Recently, I was in Greece filming a TV show with a group of overweight people. Every day I gave one-to-one sessions to the participants. Neil's session was particularly memorable. Before coming on the show he'd described himself a 'miserable git'. He was quiet and not very active. A couple of days after our session one of the participants came up to me and said, 'What on Earth did you do to Neil?' 'I don't know, what do you mean?' 'He's going round shouting, "It's a miracle!" He's banging on about feeling really confident and has turned into Action Man!'

> A few weeks ago I was giving a public talk. At the end, a girl came up to me and said, 'My friend came on your course two years ago. She's married to a guy she met on the course. When I found you were giving this talk, I thought I'd come and see for myself. My friend said you were one of the funniest, most charming, nicest people she'd ever met.' I was flattered that someone should pay me such a lovely compliment.

What's the difference between that story and this:

> I appear on TV and travel abroad as part of my work. The work I do has remarkable effects on some people, from confidence-building to removing phobias. I give after-dinner talks and travel abroad to run seminars and I'm charming, funny and nice.

Both are telling you about the kind of person I am, my skills and my status in the world, but the effect isn't the same. People reading the second paragraph might bristle at what appears to be boastful to them. It's also less credible because I am telling you about myself whereas the previous paragraph is a 'testimony' of a third party – it has much more 'cred'!

Try it out for yourself and see!

What I Want

Compare these two descriptions:

> The role of personal assistant is very important. You will be expected to liaise with clients and take bookings for courses. Your job is to make the clients feel good and encourage them to train with us. You will also be required to do personal stuff for me. The hours are varied and you can work part time by negotiation.

■   ■   ■

> Tony, my last personal assistant, was a gem. Once when he was handling an enquiry about our courses, I overheard him telling the client what a lovely voice she had. She didn't book on the course, but Tony promised to get her the phone number of a dance trainer I recommended. He rang her back a day later and by the time he'd finished the call, she had booked. She told me that she really appreciated him taking the trouble to find the dance teacher's number, especially when she hadn't even booked. Tony always came to my seminars whenever he could, even though it wasn't in his job description. He even found someone to look after my dog for a couple of weeks when I was on holiday.

How much more information do you get about what's expected in the job when you hear Tony's story?

Characters

Stories don't just tell us about the people we meet or the jobs we might do. They also teach us about life's lessons. Films and stories are full of characters who do just this. For example, we often talk about people as being 'just like 'Joey from *Friends*'. Popular culture is familiar to people so when you use well-known characters or stories, they can relate to it. Trainers often quote from films and TV shows because they know it's a great way to get a message across:

> 'I was watching *Fatal Attraction* last night. Boy, is that scary! It's amazing how just one lapse can lead to so much horror. The sad thing was that Michael Douglas's character loved his wife and kids and had a good marriage. If only more people would *stop* for a moment and realize the value of what they have and what they might lose.'

> *Message:* Having a fling is a dangerous business if you have agreed on monogamy. Think first. Are you prepared to risk everything you love for a moment's pleasure?

> 'Did you ever see that film with Harrison Ford, where he was searching for the Holy Grail? I love that bit where he is told to take a step from the edge of the ravine and there's nothing but a 300 ft drop beneath him. Isn't it great when he puts his foot out and the bridge suddenly appears from nowhere?'

> *Message:* Sometimes when you take a major step into the unknown, you get help from unexpected quarters. You just have to *trust* in the process and *everything will work out.* Harrison Ford's character was scared, but he trusted and took the step and reaped the rewards.

Ancient mythologies, novels, films and TV are overflowing with scenes and characters that can be used as learning and teaching tools. You will also find stories in newspapers and day-to-day life. Be on the lookout for stories that have a lesson woven in.

You can find out a lot about people when you know what stories attract them. Many of us particularly relate to heroic characters. What stories or characters do you relate to? How does this affect the way you live your life? What fictional character embodies a special way of being you'd like access to?

Sam said that she really related to Little Red Riding Hood. She even had a red cape and a pair of shoes that she called her 'Red Riding Hood shoes'. When she thought about why she related to Little Red Riding Hood, she suddenly realized that she was always being distracted along the path too.

If you want an insight into someone, ask them which historic or heroic figure/s they relate to and why. You'll uncover all sorts of interesting information. Me, I'm a Wonderwoman fan! She embodies power and femininity in one sexy package.

Quotes

Quotes are so inspiring. The right ones at the right time just seem to have a way of uplifting, moving and motivating you.

People trust quotes when they're from books or from a reliable source – 'my grandmother always used to say', 'a lawyer friend told me'; 'I read a survey in *New Scientist* which indicated ...'

For example, my grandma always used to say, 'Just when you're about to give up, something always turns up.' It's true, isn't it? And because grandmothers are seen as kind, wise, trustworthy people, who wouldn't be open to a message from someone like that?

Believe me, quotes are a great way to get a message across. Notice how empowering you find the quotes in this book.

I just love that quote by Marianne Williamson that says:

> Our deepest fear is not that we are inadequate. Our deepest fear is that we are powerful beyond measure ... there is nothing enlightened about shrinking so that other people won't feel insecure around you.

That's a good one to remember. And here are a couple more gems ...

Two Gems That Everyone Should Know
HOW TO GIVE LOVING CRITICISM

> Treat people as if they were what they ought to be and you help them to become what they are capable of being.
>
> **Johann Wolfgang von Goethe**

When you're content with yourself and know who you are and what's right for you, criticism doesn't pierce your heart. *But* we're all a work in progress and criticism isn't always easy to take. It is associated with censure, disapproval, disparagement, condemnation and denigration. No wonder it's a very sensitive topic.

Sadly many 'critics' don't take the time to lubricate but just dive straight in. That can hurt. Bear that in mind before you begin to criticize someone.

When you feel a criticism coming on, stop and ask yourself what is the purpose of it. Is it designed to help the person it's directed towards? If it isn't, then what are you trying to do? Are you trying to satisfy yourself or put them down? Criticism has only one purpose in my rules: to help someone to do something better or to improve themselves. Let me tell you a story about that.

I had just finished a training session as part of my interview as a freelance trainer for Happy Computers and Henry, the founder of the company, asked me, 'What did you do well?'

I started to ramble on about how I didn't think I'd done too well getting across one particular concept. He stopped me and said, 'I asked you what you did *well*. Don't tell me about what went wrong. *What did you do well?*'

It felt really good to focus on the things that I had done well and when it came to answer the next question, it was easy. The next question offered me the chance to think of the things I might have seen as mistakes and work out what I might do differently next time.

Henry used this technique with all his staff and Happy Computers lived up to its name. It really was a very happy, nurturing and fun place to work.

When you are criticizing people from a position of power, whether as a parent or a teacher or in business, it's important to lead them to their own realizations. Self-awareness has more impact and is more likely to get results. Give people the chance to say how they'd change things too and they will feel empowered. And in return you will receive their loyalty and respect.

No matter what you do, though, you will come across people who are so sensitive that they buckle at the first whiff of criticism. In cases like this there's an old training technique that works wonders. I think of it as the 'Kiss, kiss, slide it in, cuddle, cuddle' technique.

Kiss, Kiss

First you find something positive to say. It could be about the person in general or specific qualities or strong points. If you're going to deliver criticism about work, for example, make it a positive statement about their work. Similarly, in a relationship it helps to start out with words like 'I love you' or 'You're very special to me.'

Slide It In

When they're feeling good, gently slide in the criticism. Keep the positive focus, know that they're doing the best they can with the resources they have available to them, send them nice thoughts and have in mind the best outcome for all. That way you'll find yourself with a smile on your face, using a gentler tone of voice and ... they'll just open out and take it in.

Cuddle, Cuddle

And when they've had a moment to absorb what you've said, you can leave them with some kind words and a smile on their face and a warm feeling inside.

Here's an example:

> Andy, you did a great job of getting the reports filed on time, and I thought you managed to cut the material down sensitively without missing the point. *I did notice that it took rather longer to finish the stats* and they had to be sent by courier separately. That's something I'd like you to pay attention to next time. You've been doing a great job overall and thanks again for all the effort you put in organizing Tom's leaving do, it was a great party.

Practise using this technique when you next feel the urge to adopt the critic's role. You'll be surprised how easy it is to subtly slide in your message when you kiss, kiss and cuddle, cuddle.

And v. But

What's the difference between how you feel when reading the two statements below? Be aware of the feelings in your body as you read.

'I like you, but you're not my type.'
**'I like you and I admire many things about you and I'm sorry that we just don't
seem to have that spark.'**

'But' is like the backspace delete key on your computer. It erases all memory of the words that went before it.

Avoid 'but' and practise using 'and'. 'And' keeps the memory of the nice things you've said and creates a nice space into which the criticism can flow. It makes the criticism feel much softer and more acceptable.

Be Disagreeable

I was listening to a debate on the radio between two people who obviously felt strongly about the subject. One of them responded regularly to the other's views by saying 'You're wrong' or 'That's complete rubbish' and proceeded to tear apart his argument. The other guy only said, 'I disagree,' and proceeded to make a case for his argument.

Instead of telling someone 'You're wrong', how about trying 'I disagree' and then telling them what you think? No need to trash anyone to put across your point!

HOW TO SAY 'NO' AND RETAIN RESPECT

As a semi-reformed 'people-pleaser' I know how hard it is sometimes to say 'no'. There's that awful scary feeling that you won't be liked or that people will be upset. But saying 'yes' when deep down you mean 'no' is very unhealthy. What usually happens is the moment you agree to something you begin to think about all the reasons why you didn't want to do it in the first place. This can rapidly turn into resentment and will certainly give your self-esteem a dent.

Patrice's husband was telling me what attracted him to her. Apart from her charisma and presence, it was her strong sense of self-worth. I know when we were younger if she'd made up her mind that something wasn't for her, no amount of girlie pleading by her friends would convince her it was. She's always expected the best for herself and has sometimes lost 'friends' through it. But that's nothing compared to the friends who are loyal to her. What we love about her is her integrity and strong sense of who she is.

How often have you said 'yes' when you meant 'no' and what were the consequences?

SAYING 'YES' AND MEANING 'NO'

- Take a piece of paper and list the occasions when you've said 'no' and meant 'yes'. It could be anything from sleeping with someone when you didn't want to to eating something that you didn't like so as not to upset the person who prepared it. Think of those moments when someone has said 'Go on' or 'Please, just for me ...'
- Beside each entry in the list write what happened as a result. What feelings did you have at the time? Did you build up resentment towards the other people?
- Notice when you feel the urge to 'give in' and quickly examine your motives. Ask yourself: 'What do I really, really want to do?'
- Check where you get the feelings. You know when something's right for you and when it isn't.
- If it isn't, just say 'no'. Use neutral but firm phrases: 'This just isn't for me'; 'I know when something's right for me and this isn't'; 'I'd like to help you and right now it's not possible.'
- And don't procrastinate. The worst thing you can do is to give someone the idea that you might say 'yes' at another time when you know you won't. When I get cold callers on the phone, I just say firmly but kindly, 'Sorry, I'm not interested, goodbye,' and I put the phone down. No need to be nasty or tell complicated lies. Deep down no salesperson worth their salt wants you to say 'yes' when you aren't really interested. They know it creates 'buyer's remorse'. When you give a straightforward answer people will respect you for your honesty. It also tells them that you can't be manipulated and you are not an easy mark.

A Word about Public Speaking

In survey after survey 'public speaking' is high on the list of people's top ten worst fears. Why are so many of us afraid of speaking out in front of people? And how can we shift that fear and learn to express ourselves freely?

WHY THE FEAR?

There are many situations that spark off this fear. You may remember incidents in school where either you or friends were humiliated whilst standing in front of the class. Or maybe you were a noisy child who was always told to sit still and be quiet. You may have been told to 'stop hogging the limelight'. So you were mistakenly programmed into believing that standing in front of people and talking is not acceptable behaviour. And later, when you are faced with similar circumstances, your feelings of fear are triggered again as the memories flood back.

If you do suffer from this kind of phobia and really want to be able to speak in public, I strongly advise you to consult an NLP practitioner (*see* Resources *on page 209)*. You will be surprised at how quickly some phobias can be banished.

PETA'S GUIDE TO COMPELLING SPEAKING

When you follow my advice, you will begin to find the thought of public speaking becoming more and more compelling.

- *Know your stuff.* When I give talks on how to attract what you want into your life, I rarely prepare. I'm very familiar with the subject, I have experience of how it's worked for me and my clients, I have a sense of where I want the audience to be at the end of my session and I know what elements I want to get across. In short, I know what I'm talking about. Use notes if it makes you feel more confident but don't feel bound by them.
- *Collect relevant stories.* Have a selection of stories or examples to illustrate what you're speaking about. Stories bring the dullest subject matter to life. Start looking out for stories. You'll be surprised how they come up through friends, on the radio, in the newspaper, on TV and in films.
- *Connect with your audience.* Before you start speaking, take a moment or two to look around and get a feel for the audience. You will notice some smiling faces and some people leaning forward. Make eye contact with as

many people as feels comfortable. The more people you connect with in this way, the more likely they are to react positively to you. Send positive thoughts to them: 'I like you. I want to connect with you. You are open to what I have to say.'

- *Stay in your body and out of your head.* Notice if you're hopping outside yourself and talking to yourself rather than being in your body and staying aware of what is happening right now. You can easily stop this once you notice it. Take a moment to get in touch with the now by focusing your mind on the point just below your navel. The audience won't notice what you're doing and it's much more effective than stumbling on.

- *Avoid the podium.* If you are asked to speak from one, find some way to stand in front of it or to the side. Standing behind a podium might feel safe to you, but you're telling your audience two things: 'I'm hiding behind here' and 'I'm apart from you.' Instead, try saying: 'They asked me to stand up here, but I just can't connect with you, so I'm going to move over here.' And if you can't move, make a joke of it and let them know you want to connect. Like this, you will develop a powerful kinship with your audience.

- *Throw away the notes and go with the flow.* This is a courageous move for many. But have you seen those speakers who stand rigidly in front of their audience, clinging to their notes? They have created an inner sense that they will be lost without the notes, i.e. they don't know what they're speaking about. Make notes if you wish, even write out a speech, but when you get out there, leave the paper and the 'Don't I look good?' powerpoint slides at home. Let it be just you and your audience.

- *Breathe, relax and access your Bliss-spot.* Know that anything is possible and that this is a great opportunity to really connect with people.

- *Speak your truth.* Always be yourself. Speaking from your heart will express itself in confident body language.

- *Acknowledge and respect your audience.* If your audience is attending voluntarily, a great line to begin with is: 'I know you've come here for a purpose or you're here for a reason.' Of course they have, and by this simple remark you've already got them agreeing with you! If they've been made to come to the talk, maybe at the expense of something they're working on, then acknowledge that by saying something like: 'I know that you have important things to do and I appreciate your taking the time out to come here today ...'

- *Rejoice in your mistakes.* Contrary to what many people think, audiences love you to make mistakes. It makes you human. There have been times when I've lost my train of thought (usually because I've stepped outside myself to have a chat with myself!) and I've stopped and smiled and said, 'I just lost track – it'll come back.' And it does. Sometimes people will remind you, and that creates kinship too. Your mistakes can become brownie points if you use them well.

Like this, public speaking is very empowering. For me it's about communing with people, sharing ideas and sparking off inspiration. With that in mind, you too can seek out opportunities to speak out in public. Speak to friendly strangers, join a speaking group, offer yourself for speaking engagements on your specialist topic, ask a question at a public meeting, stand up and make a speech at a leaving do, be the first to congratulate someone in public, try out karaoke ... The opportunities are endless. And great public speakers have an aura about them that's irresistible ...

And now it's time to put it all into action! Get ready to turn the page and go for it ...

CHAPTER 7

ATTRACTION ACTION

The goal is to live life with godlike composure on the full rush of energy like Dionysus riding the leopard without being torn to pieces.

Joseph Campbell

Remember how at the beginning of this book, I talked about the qualities of attractive people? Let me remind you of them once again.

- They like themselves.
- They know what they want and expect to get it.
- They are happy and positively upbeat.
- They are confident without being arrogant.
- They don't *need* other people to make them happy, but people genuinely like them and actively seek their company.
- They are enjoying the adventure of their life, not just watching it pass by.
- They are successful and fulfilled in what they do, whether it's being a roadsweeper or a doctor.
- They are emotionally and spiritually mature.
- They have empowering belief systems that inspire optimism, excitement and determination.
- They have a strong sense of integrity and know what's right for them.
- They are able to be open and vulnerable because they have a resilient inner core.
- They sail through stormy challenges to calmer, more fruitful seas.

- They can laugh at themselves and life.
- They do things for other people without constantly thinking, 'What's in it for me?'
- They are able to surf the roughest waves on life's ocean.
- They see the potential in others.
- They speak positively of other people.
- They are loyal and caring.
- They want to see everyone win.
- They have well-developed social skills.
- They move and speak elegantly.
- They are exciting to be with.
- They are sexually mature and confident.
- They have an almost hypnotic 'follow-me' quality and make great leaders.
- They are highly flexible and can easily adapt to others without giving up their own sense of self.
- They are in tune with their intuition.
- They seem to attract what they want without effort.
- They experience 'failure' as a lesson on the path to success.
- Their bodies reflect all this with a sense of calm, a readiness for action and free-flowing uninhibited movement.

Know that you have the power to develop all these qualities. Their potential is a seed inside you waiting for you to nurture it and bring it to fruition. Let's look at how you can activate your attraction power.

ACTIVITIES TO BOOST YOUR ATTRACTION POWER
Your Personal Oath of Allegiance

We make all sorts of vows and oaths and mostly they're related to someone or something else. Doesn't it make sense to start with pledging allegiance to *ourselves*?

It might go something like this:

> As a member of the world I acknowledge that in order to fulfil
> my role in the world I have a duty first to myself. To this end I do
> solemnly swear that to the best of my ability I will endeavour to
> live my life according to these guidelines:

I love myself completely and absolutely.

I believe in myself.

I am totally committed to myself.

I am true to myself.

I follow my dreams.

I want what's best for myself.

I look after myself.

I am alert and notice things.

I pay attention to my body.

I am studying and learning about myself.

I forgive myself.

I am patient with myself.

I look for possibilities.

I encourage myself.

I excite myself.

I congratulate myself.

I expand my horizons.

I ask for help when I need it.

I am in the here and now.

I pick myself up and start all over again.

I am grateful for my gifts.

I will apply all these thoughts to other people too.

SWEARING YOUR OATH

- You can make up your own personal oath of allegiance or adapt the above. Make it really special. Let it encompass all that you desire to be.
- Print it out and place it up somewhere you can see it every day. Laminate it, make it attractive in any way that works for you.
- Learn it by heart and repeat it often to yourself – and before you go to bed at night say it as a vow of how you will be tomorrow.

Polish your Intuition

The intuitive mind is a sacred gift and the rational mind is a faithful servant. We have created a society that honours the servant and has forgotten the gift.

Albert Einstein

Paul Bauer, founder of A Dream's Alive, a company devoted to helping people follow their dreams, says:

> Your intuitive mind isn't up in your head – it's based in your heart and your gut. In fact, people like Einstein were considered *incredibly intelligent* – but not because their brains were so advanced. What made them *so intelligent* was they used their 'intuitive mind', as Einstein calls it, and learned to trust their *heart* and their *gut* feelings.
>
> If you ever feel like you're struggling, *you're using your rational mind.* You've fallen into 'honouring the servant' instead of listening to and *trusting* the gift.

We all have powerful intuitive potential, but our intuitive abilities often lie dormant through lack of use. When you polish your intuition you gain greater access to your own hidden knowledge as well as pick up on the micro-signals being sent out by other people. That makes intuition a great awareness tool.

The good news is that we can all wake up our intuition with a little practice. As with any new skill that you take on, you have to devote time to it and exercise it from time to time to get it into action. But here are some ways that have helped many people, including me, to become much more intuitive.

TAP INTO YOUR ENERGY CENTRES

You may have heard of energy centres in the body, known as chakras. The chakra system has been around almost forever and forms the basis for most Eastern medicine and healing systems as well as martial arts and bodywork. It is also a tried and tested model for interpreting your feelings. So, when you're having feelings in particular areas of your body, you might find it useful to check them out against the table of chakras below. It will give you some idea of which area of your life you need to work on.

Chakra	Location	Colour	Associated with	Possible Problems
Root	At the base of your body, between your legs. When you sit down, imagine it's the bottom of a coil going up and through the middle of your body	Red	Survival, basic needs, belonging, putting down roots The physical world Having	Lack of stability, need to put down roots, feeling disconnected from the world
Sacral	Between your belly button and the top of your pubic bone, in the middle of your body	Orange	Creativity, sexuality, desire, self-determination, personal power Wanting	Feelings of powerlessness, lack of creativity or direction, sexual-based problems
Solar plexus	In your gut, midway between your heart and your belly button	Yellow	Self-worth, confidence, understanding, sympathy, compassion Feeling and ability	Gut feelings, intuition nagging, other people's sorrow, lack of confidence, feeling unworthy, incapable
Heart	You got it – it's located in your heart area	Pink or green	Loving and being loved, self-love, joy, balance, unconditional love Loving	Lack of love, finding it difficult to give or receive love Loss of love
Throat	Yes, another easy one. It's in your throat area	Blue	Self-expression, freedom, communication, expansion Speaking out	Feeling you're being heard, not saying what you mean, fear of public speaking

Chakra	Location	Colour	Associated with	Possible Problems
Brow	On the forehead between the eyebrows	Indigo/dark blue	Clairvoyance, vision, spiritual awareness, intuitive thinking, the third eye Seeing beyond	Confusion
Crown	Top of your head	Violet	Universal connectedness, the divine, spiritual awareness, sense of something beyond self Knowing	

It is claimed that when you clear your chakras, energy flows more freely around your body and you are much more open to noticing things that might otherwise be beyond your awareness.

Try it with this exploration. It's fun and the very least you'll get from it is a sense of balance or calm!

LETTING YOUR ENERGY FLOW

- Take some quiet time and sit comfortably in a chair, or cross-legged if you want to, though it's not actually obligatory to sit. You can even do this whilst washing up.
- Get into deep belly breathing.
- Focus your attention on each chakra area one by one. Imagine you're breathing into the chakra and think of the positive qualities associated with that chakra.
- Notice how the feelings change in that area.

Here are some hints to get you started:

Base chakra: **Get a sense of being connected, part of a group, family or organization.**
Sacral chakra: **Sense your personal power, your creativity and your desires. (This is a juicy one!)**
Solar plexus: **Know that you are valuable and you are special in your own unique way.**
Heart: **Feel that you are loving and loved.**
Throat: **Hear yourself speak your truth and communicate freely.**
Third eye: **Sense yourself noticing things you didn't pick up on before.**
Crown: **Know you are part of something marvellous, something much greater than yourself.**

- When you get to the crown, just imagine energy looping back down to your base and back up again.

Enjoy!

ASK FOR ANSWERS

Do you ever get those times when you just don't know what to do? Your head spins with thoughts of this and that and you end up feeling confused.

Sometimes you need more information to make a decision. At other times, you can be pretty sure that you already have your answer, but your thoughts are muddying your mind and hiding it from you.

To clear your mind, try the following explorations.

SLEEP ON IT

- Try using your sleep to get clarity.
- Make a list of all the 'I don't know what to do' things in your life.
- Before you go to bed each night, practise some deep belly breathing, let your mind go quiet and simply ask for an answer. Go to sleep with that in mind.

THE OVEN OF POSSIBILITY

- Another way of doing this is to create an imaginary 'oven of possibility' at the back of your mind.
- Take one 'problem' a day and decide to let go of worrying about it and just put it in the 'oven of possibility' to cook for 24 hours. You'll be surprised how answers just come.

With both methods, only work on one problem at a time!

Answers often pop up as a 'knowing', accompanied by a good feeling in your body. They may come in at any time, so the more time you spend in the present, free of thought clutter, the more space you are giving for answers to come out.

RUPERT'S WOODLAND WALK

Nature is one of the best places to develop your intuitive skills. Tuning into nature is a great way to become aware of how your body picks up messages and nature is also a great teacher in letting things unfold the way they are meant to. It's the ultimate lesson in patience.

Rupert Soskin of the School of Insight and Intuition in southwest London takes people into a local wild park to help them tune into the subtle signals that surround us so abundantly in nature. On the day I accompanied them, everyone had a unique experience. Wherever you are, you can try it out for yourself with the following exploration.

A WALK IN NATURE

Go for a walk in a park or somewhere that has trees and open spaces – the more variety, the better. As you walk, pay attention to your body. Notice the trees. Does one in particular seem attractive to you? If so, walk up to it slowly, continually noticing the sensations. Stand with your back against it, or touch it with your hands, or put your forehead on it. Notice any sensations you get. Try walking slowly away from the tree. Then try it with another tree. Notice what's different about being in a group of trees and then out in the open.

If you want to, hold out the palms of your hands towards what you want to sense. This helps some people. Everyone senses things differently – just notice what happens to *you.*

As you walk, take some time to tone up your senses. Pay attention to the sounds. Imagine you are hearing them with different parts of your body, like your back or your feet. Notice what that feels like. Then concentrate on the sights. Move your eyes around. Pay attention to colour, shading, light and darkness, brilliance and dullness. Notice the changes in your body as you look at different things.

And be on the alert for those moments when you slip out of the present moment and onto a thought train. Then bring yourself back.

Wherever you are, the more you focus your attention on what's happening in your body, the more easily you'll be able to pick up signals from the world around you. Notice how you react around certain people, in different people's homes, in particular locations. Notice what feels good and what feels uncomfortable. How do you react to sounds, images? Pick up on the subtle signals and listen to them. They hold valuable information for you.

Be Nice to People for No Good Reason

One of the greatest activities of all time is being nice to people for no good reason. I shall always remember the first time I heard this phrase at an NLP training with Richard Bandler. I was to hear it many times after that. And isn't it a great way to live?

Here are some ways you can bulk up your 'nice' muscles.

WHAT'S GREAT?
- Focus your mind on your heart or get a sense of love and imagine sending it to the person you are checking out. (This makes it much easier to notice the good stuff.)
- What do you really like about this person? What positive qualities do they have? Let them come up, and if negative qualities come, just acknowledge that they exist and continue your search for the good stuff.

- Which of their positive qualities don't you have? How can these qualities benefit you?
- If you notice any negative qualities, are they a reflection of how you are sometimes? (Be honest here!)
- Assuming you can't change anything, on balance does the positive outweigh the negative or vice versa?
- If you feel more positive about the person now, make sure you communicate that to them. Imagine there's a hotline from your heart to theirs and just look at them. Do this often.
- And when they irritate you or do things you don't like, try looking at them and thinking, 'They're a human being with flaws just like me,' *and smile.*

A GOOD DEED A DAY

- Resolve to do a good deed every day for at least a week and then notice what happens. Here are some ideas to get you going:

Smile at someone you don't know and say hello.
Open a door for someone.
Let someone out in traffic.
Invite the neighbours in for a drink.
If you don't know your neighbours, introduce yourself to them and take them a small gift.
Pay someone a compliment.
Go out of your way to help someone.
Give someone your place in the queue.
Let someone else get the empty seat on the train.
Call someone who'd like to hear from you and resolve to uplift them.
Make someone smile.
Buy someone you care for a surprise gift.

There are endless things you can do when you fire up your imagination.

- When you've done the deed, remind yourself about it by saying something like 'That's another good deed for the day.'

- When you get a good reaction from someone, check your feelings. Mentally pat yourself on the back and feel good for having put some sparkle into the world. Remember that 'sparklers' are very attractive.
- At the end of the day, write your good deeds down in your attraction diary.

MAKE UP EXCUSES DAY

- Pick a day and decide that no matter what someone does to you, you're going to come up with several explanations for their behaviour. For example, say a driver cuts you up in traffic and then beeps you as if it's your fault. Instead of reacting by matching his anger, ask yourself, 'I wonder what could have happened to make him behave like that?' Come up with at least four excuses. Here are a few to get you going:

His partner left him the night before.
He's just had a puncture and he's covered in oil and is late for a job interview.
He's behind in his mortgage payments and is living under the cloud of repossession.
His kid has been playing truant from school.
She's just found out she's got a heart problem.
Her parents never praised her.
His mother held him back.

- Keep on making up excuses or reasons for their behaviour until you run out of ideas. Go wild, let your imagination flow. These excuses don't make the person's behaviour right. But they make you more understanding of the enormous stress some people live with.
- When you've made up your excuses or reasons, send a friendly message in your mind to the person you believe has offended you. Sending out nice thoughts will creates much nicer feelings in your body than anger or rage or any other negative emotion.
- Notice any resistance that you may have put up to doing this. Be aware of the feelings you generate as you do so.
- Notice any positive thoughts you had as a result of thinking about this exploration.
- Make a note in your attraction diary.

The very least that will happen with this exercise is that it'll put you in a better frame of mind and decrease the chances of your inflicting the same behaviour on someone else. At best you'll find how much easier life is when you stop reacting and let go.

How much more attractive do you feel when you're being forgiving and letting go of negative emotions?

YOUR ATTRACTION TEMPLATE
Generate your Attraction Template

This idea was inspired by the work of Stacey Hall and Jan Brogniez, authors of *Attracting Perfect Customers: The Power of Strategic Synchronicity.*

What is an attraction template? It is a structure and process you can use for attracting *anything* you want into your life. If you're thinking about changing your career or moving home or moving on from or into a relationship, it will give you clarity on what's important to you and it will make it much more real. You will unconsciously begin to seek out the qualities and features you want, and you will find it natural to reject those that don't match.

MAGIC IN ACTION?

Gina had been thinking for some time of moving from London to Brighton. When she started looking for a home, she just thought about what she could afford and got information on everything. She looked at a lot of places, but nothing felt quite right.

When Gina created her attraction template, she had to think of all the things she wanted in a home. I asked her to write down everything that came up, without censoring it. I then took her list and asked her to consider each of the items one at a time and notice what feelings she was getting in her body and where. I asked her to look out for particularly good feelings. These would be her top priorities.

The first thing she came up with was 'outside space'. I asked her what that would give her. She talked about being able to be in touch with nature, to entertain, and so on. The feelings were located in her root area, at the base of her spine, and in her heart, so I asked her what feelings she had in relation to this garden and her sense of belonging and her heart. She told me that this space symbolized 'putting down roots, belonging and being a place where love could flourish'. We get quite poetic when we start accessing what's really important to us.

Gina finally prioritized all the items she'd come up with. She had 54! I asked her to look at the top five and ask herself what it would be like if she didn't have them. This showed her what she absolutely had to have. I then got her to create some personalized affirmations around what she wanted (see next exercise) and advised her to start telling everyone what she wanted.

Gina had a good friend, Nicky, living in Brighton, which was one of the many reasons why she'd selected that area. When she told her friend what she was planning, Nicky said, 'The flat next door to us has been on the market for 14 months. It's got a great garden, a large living area and perfect neighbours – us!'

Gina immediately called and arranged a viewing. And even if this flat didn't work out, she knew she'd find the place that was right for her because she'd got such a clear sense of it.

HOW TO GENERATE YOUR ATTRACTION TEMPLATE

Do this exercise for anything you want to attract into your life. It really works – I've used it myself many times to magnetize people and opportunities into my life.

- Get a piece of paper or a page in a large notebook and write at the top: 'My perfect job/partner/mate/home/[whatever you want to attract] has these qualities.'
- Then start making your list. Don't censor yourself.
- If any negatives come up, turn them around. If you come up with 'I don't want to live in a busy road', ask, 'What sort of street *do* I want to live in?' Let your list flow, keep going. And you can always add more later!

- Look at each item in turn and ask: 'How will this add to my life? How will I benefit? What will it give me?'
- As you do so, check your feelings. Locate them and notice whether you like them or not. You may get some 'queasy' feelings. Look at the chakra table above to help you understand what might be causing these feelings. If you have an uncomfortable feeling, is it because you don't really want this or is it just that you're scared of or unfamiliar with it?
- Prioritize your items according to the feelings. If two items feel equal, give them the same priority rating.
- Write out a paragraph about what you want, starting: 'The job/partner/mate/home that is right for me right now will be ...' and finish by adding some words that summarize what you want. Put in as much detail as you like.
- And now ask yourself: 'Now that I know what I want in my perfect job/partner/mate/home, what qualities would my perfect job/partner/mate/(and even) home expect from me?' This makes you think about how you have to be to attract what you want. Don't try to analyse this question, just notice what comes up.
- Then ask: 'What has to happen for me to attract this perfect job/partner/mate/home?' Make a list of everything that comes up. Things like 'I have to get the deposit' or 'I have to be more even-tempered' will give you an idea of what areas to work on. This list can form the basis of your action plan.

Act-ivating your Attraction Template

Now you have this wonderful concept on paper or on your computer, read it every day. Type up a copy of it in a nice font, print it out and stick it up on your wall. Take a copy of it with you to work or carry it with you on a journey. Take it out and read it often. And you can activate it by acting it out in your head.

If you were going to make a film in which everything on your attraction template suddenly appeared in your life, what would it be like? I invite you to imagine that you are now the director of your own Hollywood blockbuster. Your movie will show the story of your life working out just the way it's meant to.

MAKING YOUR MOVIE

■ Imagine your attraction template is the script for your movie. Now you are going to bring it to life. You have access to scenery, props, people – whatever you need to make it right.

Location: Where is this movie taking place? Which country, area, building ...? Choose a location that's just right for you. And remember you can have lots of different locations.

Props: If clothes turn you on, make sure you create a perfect wardrobe for yourself. What other things might be around you? Bring in any prop you think will make it more realistic.

Special effects: Pick the best sound and special-effects technicians so that you get this movie exactly as you want it.

Script: Using your template to guide you, write a script for your story. Start it from right now. You've got something that's waiting to come into your life. You know there's more out there for you. You hear the call, you dither, then something comes in to guide you, you take the leap and loads of magical things come into your life to help you. You face some trials or challenges and you win through and you get the girl, or the job or the life you deserve and walk off into the sunset.

People: What other characters will be in the movie with you? What part will they play? Be sure to write in some 'magic helpers', even if you don't know who they are yet. They will take their cues from you – you are the star of this movie. What will life be like for you right at the start of the movie, just before you begin your adventure? What's great about you? Which of your strengths will help you on your journey? If you don't think you have them yet, just write in the ones you are developing!

The happy ending: Think of how you want to feel when you've been through this adventure and have come out wiser, richer and happier. Make sure you leave things open for a sequel.

■ You are now about to direct your own movie. Before you go to sleep, or when you're in the shower, or whenever you have some time to relax, take some time and just start to let this movie run through. Make sure it's as if you're seeing it through your own eyes, *not* watching yourself. That disconnects you from it. Get connected. Step into the movie. Now let it run and enjoy it. Go right through to the happy ending.

■ When you come back from your reverie, imagine it's a month after the happy ending. What have you learned about your adventure and what has it brought to you? Write it down or say it out loud to yourself in the mirror.

Activating a dream activates the will to realize the dream. And you may find that dreams *do* come true and you can attract whatever is perfect for you.

THE JOY OF NETWORKING

> Networking means sending out into the system what we have and what we know, and having it return to recirculate continually through the network.
>
> **Wayne Dyer**

What comes to mind when you think of 'networking'? It might conjure up the image of that 'pushy' person who's at every event, distributing their business cards like confetti at a wedding. You probably know the type – when they talk to you it seems more like a hard sell than a conversation. These people give networking a bad name. My concept of networking is *very* different.

Networking is a very juicy and fruitful activity. Donna and Sandy Vilas, authors of *Power Networking*, describe it as 'people empowering people'. I like that notion. When you network, you get to meet a variety of interesting and like-minded people and have the opportunity to connect and share and offer mutual help. I'll give you an example.

Recently I was invited to take part in a debate on national radio about whether relationship books were good for you or not. I had an initial moment of annoyance because the car had come too early and then after a long journey I had to wait half an hour before I went on air. And then I changed the thought to 'Something else is going to happen, something useful.'

I went round the corner to pick up a paper and met the person I was debating with, Dr Petra Boynton, a research psychologist and sex columnist in *Men's Health*. I'd heard of her and wanted to meet her. I introduced myself and she told me that she'd been doing research into relationship books and one of her colleagues had recommended mine. 'You should meet him,' she said.

After the debate, as we were taking the lift together, I thought, 'I bet she'd love to come to the Women in Journalism party.' When I mentioned it, she smiled and told me that was great because she'd been thinking of expanding her work in journalism.

A connection was made. Respect and admiration were exchanged and we both realized that we could help each other.

Whenever you find yourself in a situation with strange people, go in with this thought in mind: 'I wonder who I might meet here who will lead me to something exciting.' You *never* know where one chance meeting can lead.

Map Out your Network

What keeps a networking connection going is two-way traffic. When you simply focus on 'What can I get out of this?', the connection will stop. So make sure the traffic goes both ways.

And with that in mind, put aside what you want to get out of networking and ask yourself: 'What do *I* have to offer?'

Don't panic – everyone has masses to offer. You know things, you know people and you have interests. You have accumulated a wealth of skills and experiences. That's plenty.

Making a network map is a great way of understanding how much you do have to offer. Try it – you'll be surprised.

MAKING A NETWORK MAP

- Take a big piece of plain paper and in the middle write your name. The paper represents the world you live in and you are the centre of it. In your universe are all the people you know. They are stars in their own universes. Think this way and this will be a fun game!
- Settle down in a quiet place and do some belly breathing. Say to yourself, 'This is going to be fun' and 'Whatever comes up will be just right.'

- Get a sense of someone you know – anyone, it doesn't matter. Write their name on the paper, anywhere around your name. This is just a draft, so don't worry. (Later you may want to do all kinds of fun things with this.)
- Next to their name, maybe in a different coloured pen, write the first thing that comes to mind about them. It could be a skill they have or someone they know, maybe 'husband works in publishing', 'is great at proofreading', 'knows a lot about nature', 'has a son who's a graphic designer', 'father is a plumber', 'goes salsa dancing', 'gets her car fixed by a great mechanic', and so on. Write it all down.
- When you have finished, let another name come to mind.
- Once you start the map, you'll find all kinds of names popping into your head. You may even find that you need a larger piece of paper!
- Place your map somewhere visible. You might like to decorate it. It is now a living, growing, organic entity. And as you encounter new people, so the map grows.

You can do this in any medium that suits you. The key is to create a resource list of people and connections that remind you just how important and useful you could be to someone.

Next time you are considering changing career or starting a new project or moving somewhere new, check your network map. It will inspire you and remind you how many magic helpers there are in your life.

Once you have a sense of how many contacts you have and how much you have to offer, you'll feel much more comfortable about networking. So it's time to get out there and get connected.

Peta's Top Tips for Networking

I've done a lot of networking in my time and learned some lessons along the way. I'd like to share the key points that I've found really useful.

REPRESENT YOURSELF AS YOU ARE

It's important to put yourself across in a way that's true to you.

There will come that time in any interaction when someone asks you, 'What do you do? The way you answer is very important.

What do you want to say about yourself? Do not feel obliged to give them your job title unless it says something about you. Think about what turns you on. 'I'm a financial planner. I love being able to give people a package that is just right for them. Did you know that [quote an interesting fact] …'

Or you can keep it short and sweet and get them curious. Rachel always says, 'I stick needles in people.' And then of course they might guess, 'Are you a nurse? Are you an acupuncturist?' It gives them an opportunity to come back. The volley has begun, and the ball flows back and forth across the net.

When I appear on TV they often put a bar across my image which describes who I am. They call this an 'Aston'. Generally I have them put 'Peta Heskell – Flirt Coach'. It makes people smile and gets them curious. It also publicises my book *Flirt Coach*. And when people type 'flirt coach' into a search engine, they find me.

Always make what you say count *for* you, not against you.

A Word about Cards

Make sure your business cards say something about you. Mine have a quote from Joseph Campbell: 'Be who you are, do what excites you, follow your bliss.' It speaks for me. My partner has a picture of a motorbike on his card and his photo. He's a bike journalist! It speaks for him. What speaks for you? What symbol, quote or design would represent who you are?

Colours can also be important. I chose a red and black card because those colours represented power and energy. My next card may have more pinks and blues and purples to represent spirituality. The colours say something about me. What do they say to you? Read up on colours and their general meanings.

USE SITUATIONAL SMALL TALK

When you're in a strange environment with a group of people, remember you're all in the same situation and if it's a party or a social event you are there for a common reason. So:

Talk about the location.
Talk about the event.

Talk about commonalities (wearing the same tie, standing alone, being tall).
Talk about the weather.
Ask for the time, directions.
Ask about someone they were talking to.

To break the ice, you could try out the following:

'**How did you get involved with/hear about this organization/club/function?**'
'**What do you think of this place? It's interesting, isn't it?**'
'**It looks as though it's going to rain.**'
'**Is this your first time here or are you an old hand?**'
'**I'm looking for ... can you help me?**'
'**I'm looking for ... do you know what they look like?**'
'**You're the only other person in the room who's as tall as me, so I thought I'd come and say hello.' (Any silly reason will do.)**'
'**I noticed you were talking to ... How did you come to know them?**'
'**Do you come here often?' Say this with a big smile on your face and in your voice!**'

Once you've set the ball rolling, the conversation will begin to flow. This creates a little rapport before you introduce yourself.

MAKE THE FIRST MOVE

Imagine this situation. You are invited to a party. Your hostess tells you that she's also inviting Y and says you two will really hit it off. You arrive at the party and your hostess is rushed off her feet. She greets you and introduces you to someone standing nearby, then rushes off with promises of 'catching up' later. You spend the evening talking to one or two people and wondering when your hostess is going to introduce you to Y. You go home feeling peeved because you never met Y.

It doesn't have to be like that.

Take the initiative. Ask your hostess to point out Y and go and introduce yourself. If he isn't there yet, ask her what he looks like. If your hostess isn't around, say to someone, 'I'm told I have to meet Y. Do you know him?' If they don't, nothing lost, if they do, you've got a topic for conversation and can find out about Y before you go over and introduce yourself to him.

Yes, that's right. *Do it yourself.* Don't rely on other people to do it all for you.

It's the same if you see someone who is familiar either because you've met them before or because you noticed them at another event. If you've met before, even briefly, go over and remind them, for example: 'Hi, I'm Tim Parks, we met at Lana's wedding/the Christmas party/the medical conference in Hawaii.' And then add in a fact about them: 'I remember you telling me you were starting a new project/getting married/moving or [whatever it is that you remember about them]. How's that going?'

If you saw them at a social event and now you're meeting in a business context, build on the connection. They will feel warmer to you knowing that you share something else in common.

If they were a speaker at an event or they did something notable, it's fine to use that as an opener, for example: 'We haven't met, but I was at your talk on ... You were speaking about ... and I was very impressed with your theories on ...'

If you want to talk about something in depth, ask them if they've got time to talk and if not, ask if it would be OK for you to contact them at a later date. Ask them which they prefer, e-mail or a phone call. You'd be surprised how many people don't feel comfortable using e-mail and love to be telephoned. Always check.

Never go up to someone you have met and say 'You won't remember me.' You're programming them to think you are an unmemorable person!

A Word about Asking People What They Do

Sometimes people love what they do and sometimes they hate it. Don't mar your conversation by encouraging someone to talk about something they'd rather avoid. When you ask them what they do and they hesitate, or twitch their mouth, they're probably not sure about their career or don't want to talk about it.

If in doubt as to whether they love their job, use the backup question: 'If you had the choice, no holds barred, what would you be doing?' This leads them to think about possibilities.

You can also use the other backup question: 'So what do you do for fun?'

If they sound enthusiastic and positive, ask them, 'Do you enjoy that?' Notice how they respond.

Keep them on the sunny side and you may be surprised at how much more open they become as they feel comfortable with you.

Share your Friends

Sharing your friends is one of the nicest ways of networking. It's empowering and rewarding. But there can be pitfalls when friends share their friends with you. Years ago I popped into a neighbour's flat for a chat. She had a few friends round and invited me in. I hit it off immediately with Denise and we spent most of the evening locked in conversation with each other. But the next day, when I called my friend to thank her for the evening, she accused me of 'hogging' *her* friends. Denise and I still see each other 30 years later, but, not surprisingly, we have both 'lost touch' with our jealous mutual friend.

It needn't be like this. If you are secure in your friends, you will want to share them with other people. It can generate positive results for all involved. And the more you do it, the more you'll find other people sharing *their* friends with *you*.

WATER YOUR GARDEN

Contacts are like seedlings growing in your garden. If you don't water and nurture them, they won't grow.

Once people have given you their cards or other contact details, transfer the most useful info into your filofax or electronic address book. Make a note of anything that's useful to know about that person.

Whenever you make a new contact, do your best to follow up fairly quickly with a call or an e-mail. Tell them you enjoyed meeting them and why. Maybe you promised to give them a number or address. Keep your promises as soon as possible after your meeting.

If you're anything like me, you receive lots of information on a daily basis. If it isn't right for you, instead of dismissing it out of hand, pass it on. Last week I saw an article in a newspaper about a designer who was giving his first collection for a big fashionwear group. He'd started by making one-offs for a local shop. I tore it out and sent it to my friend Patrice, who was just about to sell her designs to a local shop. My gesture said, 'You can make it too.'

People love that kind of thing. It's so simple and it says, 'I know what you like and I'm thinking of you.'

BE OK ABOUT ASKING

Many people feel that it's pushy or forward to ask for things. This is something I've been shaking off for a long time. Now I've realized that it's OK to ask for things.

If you ever hear yourself saying 'I don't like to ask' or 'They might take offence' or 'What if they say no?' or 'It's too pushy', beware! You've got a holdback virus in your system. Left to its own devices, it will bring your system to a halt. When you quarantine the virus and leap forward, you'll notice the difference.

Think karma. Karma means what goes around comes around. It won't always be direct, but you'll get it in some form or other and from some source or other. You ask Fred for help and you give help to Mary and Mary does a good deed for Tom and Tom helps Fred, and so on and so on. Karma makes the world go round.

When you know that you'll have your chance to repay a kindness somewhere sometime, it makes it easy to ask. So what do you ask for?

Ask for what you need.
Ask for help.
Ask for a discount.
Ask for information.
Ask for opinions (but not too often).
Ask for clarity.
Ask for meaning.
Ask for contacts.
Ask for an introduction.
Ask for an invitation (but be prepared to be OK about getting a no).
Ask for a meeting, a quick chat, five minutes, a phone call ...
Ask for directions.
Ask for guidance.
Ask for understanding.
Ask for reassurance.
Ask for lenience.
Ask for whatever it is that you want.

And keep asking, because someone somewhere will want to walk your dog, listen to you, put you in touch with someone, give you some time, lend you transport, be sympathetic to your situation and introduce to someone you want to meet ... The possibilities are endless.

AND FINALLY ...
An A–Z of Attraction

Now you've come this far, you'll be aware of all the wonderful possibilities ahead of you.

Just for fun and to remind you of some of the secrets of attraction, I've compiled an A–Z of attraction. Enjoy!

Appreciate your unique talents.
Be nice to everyone, including yourself.
Communicate with care.
Direct your focus.
Envision what you want.
Flaunt your charm.
Go where your heart leads.
Have faith in your ability to attract.
Imagine the possibilities.
Just be your wonderful self.
Keep on going.
Laugh and smile loads.
Make connections with new people.
Notice what's going on.
Observe the beauty in others.
Play often.
Quit worrying if you can't change it.
Reach out and touch.
Send out those sexy vibes.
Titillate, lubricate, insert.
Unwind and take it easy.
Venture beyond what you think is possible.
Walk in someone else's shoes.
Yawn because it's time to ...
Zzzzzzzzzzzzzzzzone out and relax.

And now we've reached the end of this particular journey, it's time for you to take off on the adventure of your life. I truly hope that this book has helped you in some way. I know I've learned heaps as I've been writing it.

If you are curious enough to want more, there is a Resources section at the back of the book listing some of my favourite tapes, books, courses and websites. And if you want to work personally with me, either privately or on a course, my details are there too.

Please e-mail me (peta@flirtcoach.com) and tell me how your life is working out. I'd be delighted to hear from you.

RESOURCES

Learning a skill is like opening a door. Though the door can be opened by another, each person must step through the doorway for themselves if they are to attain mastery of that skill.

Highly Recommended

The books, tapes and courses listed below have profoundly affected my life and have been major turning-points in my development and my way of thinking. I heartily recommend them.

BOOKS

Please note that most of these books can be ordered through amazon.co.uk or amazon.com without knowing the ISBN number or the publisher.

Carol Adrienne, *The Purpose of your Life*
If you in any way feel that you have a purpose in life that you have not yet discovered, or if indeed you do have a purpose and want to be sure about it, this book will guide you through a process of self-discovery that is truly empowering.

Richard Brodie, *Virus of the Mind*
If you want to know more about how people get mentally programmed by ideas and how to program yourself for more useful beliefs, read this book!

Dr Larry Dossey, *Be Careful What You Pray For – You Might Get It*
Larry Dossey, an American medical doctor, examines the hefty evidence in
favour of the power of thought to hex and also to cure. If you are in any way
interested in how belief systems are formed and how powerful your words can
be, read this book. It may save your life, or someone else's.

Malcolm Gladwell, *The Tipping Point*
What creates that magic moment when ideas or products take off overnight.

Stacey Hall and Jan Brogniez, *Attracting the Perfect Customer*
This is one of the best books I've read in a long time. It's encouraging,
motivating and the process is simplicity itself. It really helps you to focus on
what you want to attract into your life and is adaptable for anything you want to
attract. Check out www.perfectcustomer.com.

George Leonard and Michael Murphy, *The Life We Are Given*
A truly comprehensive personal development programme for those who are in
it for the long term.

Diane K. Osborn (ed.), *Reflections on the Art of Living: A Joseph Campbell
Companion*
This book presents, in a simple form, Campbell's basic philosophy. A treasure
trove of ways of living that allow you to flourish as *you*. A wonderful book.

Candace Pert, *Molecules of Emotion*
Candace Pert proved scientifically that emotion can be formed in cell structures
– that we do indeed form 'molecules of emotion'. A useful reference for the
scientifically minded and an interesting story of a woman's struggle in the male-
dominated world of science.

James Redfield, *The Celestine Prophecy*
This makes so much sense. It will have an effect on you.

James Redfield, *The Tenth Insight: An Experiential Guide*
You don't have to have read *The Celestine Prophecy* to learn from this book.
A fully rounded self-help book that helped me through some challenging times.

Barbara Sher, *Wishcraft*

This was the first book that really opened me out to the possibility that I could live the life I love and love the life I live. I recommend all her other books too.

Eckhart Tolle, *The Power of Now*

Tolle sets out a simple formula for letting go of harmful thoughts and staying present. It is, he says, the key to being able to fully enjoy life for what it is. I listened to this on tape. It's great 'long journey' listening.

Neale Donald Walsch, *Conversations with God*

In this worldwide bestseller, Walsch has opened to the world at large the thoughts that many of us have had for years: there is more out there and there are better ways of living. I recommend the whole *Conversations with God* series.

TAPES

Jerry and Ester Hicks, *The Abraham-Hicks Tapes*

These tapes set out some very logical ideas about the laws of the universe. They helped me get through some trying times. There is also a great website with articles and a monthly newsletter: www.abraham-hicks.com.

COURSES

These courses have all profoundly affected my life.

Insight – Opening the Heart

If you have uncleared emotions due to an unloving childhood or unhealed relationships, or are inclined to be a bit of a victim, this course offers a safe place to really become aware of limiting behaviour and start to love yourself again. A good beginner's personal development course.

Insight Seminars UK
Lonsto House
Princes Lane
London N10 3LU
Tel: 0208 883 2888
Fax: 0208 883 5533
e-mail: enquiry@insight-seminars.org.uk

Insight: Worldwide
www.insight-seminars.org

Insight: America
New England: www.insightboston.org
New Mexico, Colorado, and parts of Texas: www.lens-insight.org
New York: www.insightny.org
Pittsburgh: http://trfn.clpgh.org/insight/seminars.html
Philadelphia: www.insightphiladelphia.org/preview.html

Insight: Australia
www.insightseminars.com.au

Paul McKenna Trainings, *NLP Practitioner course*
Tel: +44 (0)20 7704 6604;
The only UK NLP Practitioner course featuring the originator of NLP, Richard
Bandler, one of my greatest teachers. Seven days of learning and *fun*. Many of
my clients have attended these courses on my recommendation and have really
expanded on what they learned from me.

Joseph Riggio, *The MythoSelf*™ *series*
www.mythoself.com
The course where I learned to be at my best and live from there – highly
recommended if you want very powerful personal change. I am still one of
Joseph Riggio's students and I continue to learn more and more as I work with
him. Courses are held in the USA and UK.

Other Recommended Books and Courses
RELATIONSHIPS

David M. Buss, *The Evolution of Desire*, Basic Books
An in-depth study of human mating behaviour. Explains a lot!

Helen Fisher, *Anatomy of Love,* Fawcett Columbine
A cross-cultural study of marriage, mating, flirting, sex, adultery and more –
very enlightening.

Bradley Gerstman, Christopher Pizzo and Rich Seldes, *What Men Want*,
HarperCollins
A fascinating insight into 30-something American male yuppies' ideas of how
women should be.

Lillian Glass, *Attracting Terrific People*
A great little workbook for helping uncover your best you.

Gay and Kathlyn Hendricks, *Conscious Loving*, Bantam
How to move your relationship from co-dependence to co-commitment.
A sensitively written workbook bursting with great ideas for couples.

Susan Jeffers, *Opening our Hearts to Men*
How to avoid dependency.

Daphne Rose Kingma, *The Future of Love*, Broadway Books
Kingma explores where relationships have gone wrong and offers a more
spiritual path to creating loving relationships in the 21st century.

Leil Lowndes, *How to Make Anyone Fall in Love with You* and *How to Talk to
Anyone*, Thorsons
Great technique books, once you get the attitude and state of mind.

Anne Teachworth, *Why We Pick the Mates We Do*
This book helps us learn far more about the personal behavioural and attraction
patterns that cause people to seek out very similar partners on a recurring basis.

SEXUALITY AND TANTRIC SEX

The Barefoot Doctor, *The Barefoot Doctor's Handbook for Modern Lovers*,
Piatkus
I left this book in my boyfriend's bathroom, which led to some interesting
developments in our sex life! An amusing read and some useful ideas.

Mantak Chia, *Taoist Secrets of Love: Cultivating Male Sexual Energy*, Aurora
Press
How men can go at it for hours and have multiple orgasms!

Mantak Chia and Douglas Abrams Arava, *The Multi-Orgasmic Man*, Thorsons
This is an ideal beginner's book on tantric sex. Its gentle introduction and focus on male needs is great for getting a man to explore this stuff. Give it as a present – it could change your sex life forever!

Richard Craze, *Tantric Sexuality: A Beginner's Guide*
I love this book. It's lighthearted and offers a simple intro to the basics of tantric sex without too much emphasis on the esoteric side.

Julia Henderson, *The Lover Within*
This is a superb little workbook for developing your sexual energy and enhancing your sexual ecstasy. I recommend it as an easy beginner's guidebook.

Phillip Hodson and Anne Hooper, *How to Make Great Love to a Man* and *How to Make Great Love to a Woman*, Robson Books
Two beautifully illustrated glossy hardback books which offer comprehensive information on every aspect of lovemaking from straight sex to whatever takes your fancy. Highly recommended.

Leora Lightwoman, *Tantra: Supremely Satisfying Sacred Sex*, Piatkus
Leora has inspired me with her approach to reaching spirituality through sexuality. She thinks of her book as a journey to the heart of sacred sex, truly harnessing sexual energy to create ways of being that go right beyond sex. If you are inspired to enhance your sexuality, read this book and check out www.diamondlighttantra.com.

Anne Moir and David Jessel, *Brain Sex*, Mandarin
Psychological, biological and genetic research into the stark difference between the male and female brains. A revolutionary book that helps to explain the male/female divide.

Dr Gabrielle Morrisey, *Urge*, HarperCollins
A veritable mine of information and advice on having the best sex life for *you*.

SPIRITUALITY

Renée Beck and Sydney Barbara Merrick, *The Art of Ritual*, Celestial Arts
A beautiful book for creating ritual for many different purposes in your life.

Thom Hartmann, *The Prophet's Way*, Hodder Mobius
The true story of Thom's spiritual awakening. A truly absorbing and easy read,
the book will touch you deeply and you will be amazed by what's possible
when someone is on their path.

Thom Hartmann, *The Greatest Spiritual Secret of the Century*,
A wonderful parable explaining simple spiritual concepts.

Michael Levin, *Spiritual Intelligence*
The byline of this book reads 'awakening the power of your spirituality and
intuition'. A fantastic book full of exercises and stuff that makes you think. Very
simply written.

Carolyn Myss, *Anatomy of the Spirit*
The seven stages of power and healing.

Carolyn Myss, *Sacred Contracts,* Harmony Books
A very comprehensive book on the roles people play, including a powerful
process that will help you to piece together the unique purpose of your life.

Leo Rutherford, *Your Shamanic Path*
Leo is one of the most respected teachers of shamanism in the UK. His books
are full of exercises and ideas to help you get more in touch with nature.

Carolyn R. Shaffer & Kristin Amundsen, *Creating Community Anywhere*,
Tarcher Putnam
A rich source of ideas on how to connect with people, offering new ways of
living and excellent guidelines on how to create your own community, ensure
positive group communication and work through conflict.

Charles T. Tart, *Living the Mindful Life,* Shambhala
This book is based around classes given by the author. It features many interactions with his students as learning examples. It's simply written with plenty of great exercises to do if you want to be more in the now.

Robert Anton Wilson, *Prometheus Rising,* New Falcon Books
This book goes a long way to explaining the ways in which we have been programmed. It will challenge many of your ideas and turn you inside-out. Don't read it if you aren't prepared to be well and truly shocked out of traditional ways of thinking!

Gary Zukav and Linda Francis, *The Heart of the Soul,* Simon & Schuster
If you want to know more about how your emotions affect you, this book is really helpful and healing.

ENERGY WORK
Books

Jack Angelo, *Your Healing Power,* Piatkus
A well-illustrated and simple step-by-step beginner's guide to developing and using your intuition and your healing energy.

The Book of Yoga, The Sivananda Vedanta Yoga Centre, available through Ebury Press
The centre is where I first learned yoga and the book is beautifully written and illustrated and covers all aspects of yoga, including its origins and spiritual side. Highly recommended.

David Carradine and Nakahara, *David Carradine's Introduction to Chi Kung,* Owl Books
This is a particularly useful companion for those who want to practise chi kung at home and who have already attended a class. If you really want to get into chi kung, though, go to a class. Look for one that is run by someone who is spiritually oriented and who weaves the philosophy in with the exercises.

Joy Gardner-Gordon, *Color and Crystals: A Journey through the Chakras,* Crossing Press, Inc.

Videos

Chi Kung with Peter Hudson, Tel. (00 44) (0) 1323 647 770 for mail order
If you can't get to a class, and you want to learn chi kung, this video by my
teacher Peter Hudson is fantastic. Filmed to the background of the sea and the
South Downs of England, it is easy to follow. Learning chi kung changed my life
in many powerful ways and it's easy to do on a regular basis.

MEDITATION AND VISUALIZATION

Shakti Gawain, *Creative Visualisation*
Simple and beautiful. The best book on visualization that I've ever read!

Helen Graham, *Visualisation: An Introductory Guide*
Use visualization to improve your health and develop your self-awareness and
creativity.

Christopher Hyatt, *Undoing Yourself with Energised Mediations*, New Falcon
Read it if you dare. This book is not mainstream, but it has some challenging
ideas and bizarre methods of shaking yourself up.

Ben Scott and Christa Michell, Tibetan Chakra Meditations
Amazing sound meditation guaranteed to free your mind and uplift you.
www.oreade.com.

DOING WHAT YOU LOVE AND LOVING WHAT YOU DO

Richard N. Bolles, *What Colour is your Parachute?*
This book is fantastic and is updated yearly. It offers lots of resources, mainly
American, but may have changed. It's great for uncovering what you love doing
and are good at doing and how to go about starting it.

Barbara Sher, *I Could Do Anything, If Only I Knew What It Was* and *Live the Life
You Love*
Barbara's books truly inspired me. They are well worth a read if you want to
make a big change and do something you've always wanted to.

INFLUENCE AND PERSUASION AND LANGUAGE
Books

Tony Buzan, *Social Intelligence,* HarperCollins
A superb little book on how to become a more socially confident person.

Robert B. Cialdini, PhD, *Influence: The Psychology of Persuasion*, Quill
A fab book on the structure and background of influence. A must for all
interested in the art of persuasion!

James Lawley and Penny Tompkins, *Metaphors in Mind: Transformation
through Symbolic Modelling*
A fascinating book on how your metaphors and symbols can be used for
personal transformation.

David J. Lieberman, PhD, *Never Be Lied to Again*, St Martin's Griffin

Patrick E. Merlevede, Denis Bridoux and Rudy Vandamme, *7 Steps to
Emotional Intelligence*, Crown House Publishing
A very detailed book about the structure of Emotional Intelligence and how to
improve it.

Susan Quilliam, *What Makes People Tick*
A really comprehensive yet simply and clearly written guide to all the different
types of people classification. Draws on NLP, psychological testing and
personality guides as well as other disciplines. Find out about yourself and the
people around you. Enlightening stuff.

Deborah Tannen, *You Just Don't Understand: Women and Men in Conversation*,
Virago, 1992
A discussion of the ways in which women and men use language differently.
Useful for improving male/female conversation.

CDs

Kenrick Cleveland, *MaxPersuasion 2000*, obtainable from
www.maxpersuasion.com
Cleveland is a master of persuasion and this is a really good CD series.

GENERAL PERSONAL DEVELOPMENT

Courses and Services

Diamond Light Tantra; www.diamondlighttantra.com
Leora Lightwoman runs splendid workshops on tantric sex from introductory
evenings to year-long courses. She runs classes in the UK with her husband and
tantric partner, Roger, a holistic doctor.

NLP Practitioners; www.nlpworld.com
Details of all NLP academies worldwide.

Love and Friends; www.loveandfriends.com
UK-based online dating site. One of the nicest UK dating sites, with a good
selection of people. My single friends highly recommend it. Also seminars and
events for members.

The School of Insight and Intuition; www.insightandintuition.com;
Richmond, London, Tel. 0208 979 0940
Great beginner's courses on intuition with Julie Soskin, plus yearly summer
courses in 'sensing the energy' with Rupert Soskin.

Nikki Slade, Free your Inner Voice; www.freeyourinnervoice.co.uk
Classes designed to fully release emotion and joy through the medium of the
voice. UK only.

Laughter clubs; www.laughteryoga.org
Find a laughter club near you.

Books

Robin Chandler and Jo Ellen Grzyb, *The Nice Factor Book*, Simon & Schuster
How to put your needs first and not live a life of wanting to be liked by everyone.

Victor Frankl, *Man's Search for Meaning*
This book is utterly inspiring. Frankl, a Jewish psychiatrist imprisoned in a concentration camp, made a study of his fellow inmates. He wanted to know what it was that kept going those who survived. If you ever feel like giving up, read this, it'll put things in perspective.

Harriet Goldhor Lerner, *The Dance of Anger*, *The Dance of Intimacy* and *The Dance of Deception*
These are totally brilliant self-development books. They are written for women, but I recommend them to men as well.

Napoleon Hill, *Think and Grow Rich*
This book has been around for years and has sold millions. It's a huge success both as a book and business and is based on the power of self-belief.

Spencer Johnson, *Who Moved My Cheese?: An Amazing Way to Deal with Change in your Work and in your Life*
This book should be compulsory for life's 'victims'. It's a great allegorical story that helps you realize that whatever comes your way, you can adapt.

Joseph O'Connor and John Seymour, *Introducing NLP*
This is the first book I ever read on NLP, the psychology behind much of what you have been learning in this book. A great technical book that gives useful information, though I advise everyone who wants to get into NLP to take a course. It's experiential, *not* intellectual.

Andy Smith, *55 Ways to Increase your Emotional Intelligence*
A super little tips booklet with loads of simple things to do that will boost your E.I.

SECRETS OF ATTRACTION

Dr Richard Wiseman, *The Luck Factor*

I love this book because Wiseman has finally proved, over eight years of carefully monitored experiments, what many people in the field of self-awareness have been saying for years: you *can* make your own luck, you *can* manifest what you want, you *can* have it all. He reveals the secrets of what makes lucky people tick, including their strategies and thought patterns, and offers some good exercises for developing your own luck factor. Highly recommended.

PETA HESKELL AND THE ATTRACTION ACADEMY AND ATTRACTION ZONE

Peta Heskell

I can be contacted via these e-mail addresses. Please feel free to write to me with any comments or questions about this book. I will do my best to ensure all electronic correspondence receives a reply.

peta@flirtcoach.com
info@flirtcoach.com
info@attractionacademy.com
or telephone (00 44) (0) 700 435 4784

The Attraction Academy

The Attraction Academy is a seminar, public-speaking and coaching organization founded by Peta to help people and organizations discover their true purpose, get what they want, foster open and loving communication, share resources, have more fun, attract perfect people and opportunities and be the best they can. Peta's perfect associate coaches have all worked with her or trained with the people she's trained with.

The Academy offers:

uniquely tailored out-of-the-box business training and coaching
a series of provocative and entertaining talks and keynotes
interactive evening talks on attraction, flirting, networking and finding your life
   purpose

Individual Personal Empowerment with Peta

Possibility Coaching for individuals and organizations

weekend and one-day training courses, including:

- 'The Flirting Weekend' – building confidence and practising communication skills in a fun setting
- 'Activate your Attraction Power' – attract your perfect partner, customer, job, lifestyle
- 'Step into the Adventure of your Life' – uncover your life's purpose and start living the life that's right for you

Check out our constantly updated website www.attractionacademy.com, which is packed full of articles on a variety of subjects, tips, solutions to problems, e-mail newsletter access, success stories, humour, workshop details and links to learning, personal discovery and self-help sites all over the world.

The Attraction Zone

The Attraction Zone is a website offering doors to all kinds of self-help, from NLP through seduction to bodywork, astrology, shamanism, healing and much more: www.attractionzone.com

FLIRT COACH

Communication Tips for Friendship, Love and Professional Success

Peta Heskell offers the key to magical communication, creating an energizing programme to help you to be yourself at your best and love it. She encourages you to see flirting as a natural life skill to use, not just in romantic relationships, but in every human interaction to make communication more personalized, more influential and more fun!

Her dynamic and innovative action plan includes:

- **Looking inside** – discover the real you and learn to revive your innate sense of child-like self-belief, curiosity, intuition and daring
- **The outside** – learn how to 'glow' become supersensitive to other people's signals, get your message across and attract the right people into your life

THE FLIRT COACH'S GUIDE TO FINDING THE LOVE YOU WANT

Communication Tips for Relationship Bliss

Flirting is a fine art – a sexy, light-hearted art that makes communication fun and has the power to transform your romantic relationships. The Flirt Coach's innovative programme helps you to examine your past relationships and understand why you pick up the mates you do.

The key to successful relationships is being able to be yourself. Flirt Coach, Peta Heskell, offers straightforward advice to help you find the love and relationships that are truly right for you by being who you are. By following Peta's programme, you can:

- Learn from past relationships and unleash your natural sexuality
- Understand and connect more deeply with other people
- Create your relationships – according to your own rules

THE LITTLE BOOK OF FLIRTING

Acclaimed flirting expert Peta Heskell's funky mini-guide to charming your way to love, friendship and success.

Peta Haskell has got flirting down to a fine art – one that can be used not just in romantic relationships but in every relationship (with teachers, neighbours, clients and colleagues) to make communication more fun. Peta insists that the key to successful socializing is being able to be yourself. This little guide is packed with tips, quotes and cheeky line drawings that will help to make you a great flirt:

- Sharpening up your senses
- Friendly flirting
- Sexual flirting
- Social events – giving out the glow
- Creating an instant rapport
- The 6 don'ts of flirting

Make
www.thorsonselement.com
your online sanctuary

Get online information, inspiration and guidance to help you on the path to physical and spiritual well-being. Drawing on the integrity and vision of our authors and titles, and with health advice, articles, astrology, tarot, a meditation zone, author interviews and events listings, www.thorsonselement.com is a great alternative to help create space and peace in our lives.

So if you've always wondered about practising yoga, following an allergy-free diet, using the tarot or getting a life coach, we can point you in the right direction.

thorsons
element